D0880847

THE HEART OF THE SALE

THE
HEART
OF THE
SALE

Making the Customer's
Need to Buy
the Key to Successful Selling

GARRY MITCHELL

amacom
American Management Association

This book is available at a special
discount when ordered in bulk quantities.
For information, contact Special Sales Department,
AMACOM, a division of American Management Association,
135 West 50th Street, New York, NY 10020.

Library of Congress Cataloging-in-Publication Data

Mitchell, Garry.
   The heart of the sale : making the customer's need to buy the key
to successful selling / Garry Mitchell.
      p.   cm.
   Includes index.
   ISBN 0-8144-5991-9 (hard)
   1. Selling.   2. Marketing.   3. Sales promotion.   I. Title
HF5438.25.M59   1991
658.8'5—dc20   *90-56190*
                                                          CIP

Printing number

10 9 8 7 6 5 4 3 2 1

Contents

INTRODUCTION   1

1 MARKETING VS. PROSPECTING   8

Mass marketers sell millions of dollars' worth of goods every day in the United States and yet they don't ever prospect. In this chapter we examine the process marketers use to find and target markets so that they don't have to make cold calls. We take the first steps toward translating this process into selling.

2 HOW TO MARKET RATHER THAN PROSPECT   22

One of the keys to marketing is developing lists of likely prospects who are ready and interested in buying. In this chapter we look at sources available to salespeople that will help them target prospects. We examine both commercially available demographics and how to develop private sources.

3 USING MARKET INFORMATION TO
   PROSPECT EFFECTIVELY   39

Even the best-targeted prospects must be contacted. Both mail and telephone are available to salespeople, and in this chapter we examine efficient ways to use them. We look at how to write an effective initial

contact letter and then how to follow it up with a
productive phone call.

**4 THE HEART OF THE SALE:
CALL OBJECTIVES**   **58**

Every contact between the salesperson and the
prospect, including both the marketing letter and the
telephone follow-up, must be shaped by the behavior of
the customer. In this chapter we look at how call
objectives are framed to describe the customer's
actions, not those of the salesperson. This is a critical
and unique process in our sales approach.

5 HOW BUYERS SEE SELLERS   **71**

At this point in the sales cycle the salesperson meets
the customer face to face. Most salespeople experience
this moment every day. But nearly always it is from
their own perspective. This chapter examines this
moment and the rest of the sales cycle from the
customer's point of view. Some interesting differences
emerge.

6 ESTABLISHING THE RIGHT RELATIONSHIP   **85**

Examining the differences in perspective between the
customer and the salesperson leads to the inescapable
conclusion that the salesperson can put that customer
at ease only by establishing a relationship of mutual
trust and benefit. In this chapter we examine the
psychological dynamics and practical skills involved in
doing so. We develop procedures for creating such
relationships. This is the first step in the face-to-face
selling cycle from the customer-oriented salesperson's
point of view.

7 QUESTIONS: THE ART OF SELLING   **114**

Strategically, in the planning phase, the objective is
the heart of the sale. But tactically, the core skill, the
heart of the actual process of interacting with the
customer, is the art of asking questions that do not
"interrogate" or alienate the prospect. We look at how

to frame such questions and at ways to develop and hone this crucial selling skill. It is the second step in the cycle. We also examine the sources of customer needs that are revealed by asking questions in the right way.

8 PRESENTING SOLUTIONS TO CUSTOMER PROBLEMS   **140**

This is the third step in the cycle and we approach it as a set of skills and "how to" steps designed to counter the potentially negative image of the sales situation harbored by the customer and to help the salesperson to make a truly persuasive and effective presentation. This step is often taken for granted and is the prime cause of many lost sales. As we see in this chapter, it needn't be.

9 NEGOTIATING THE TERMS OF THE SOLUTION PRESENTED   **153**

Most sales literature refers to this, the fourth step in the cycle, as "handling objections." A better way to regard it is as negotiating and tailoring the sale. We look in this chapter at what goes into an effective negotiation and how the salesperson can help customers to satisfy their need to buy.

10 CLOSING FROM THE FIRST MOMENT OF CONTACT   **167**

No salesperson can make a sale without making some form of close, the final step in the sales cycle. In fact many of the sales that fail to come to fruition do so because of the manner in which the salesperson attempts (or fails to attempt) the close. In this final chapter we look at the differences between aggressive selling and assertive selling and we examine the three most polished professional skills of selling.

APPENDIX: A Selection of Sources of Prospecting Information   **180**

INDEX   **193**

THE
HEART
OF THE
SALE

Introduction

That phone system in the outer office looks like it must have been made in the 1950s, Dickerson thought as he was ushered into the office of Mr. Wright, the senior partner in Wright, Wright, and Jayston, Inc.

Dickerson sold telephone systems and he knew a good prospect when he saw one.

"Good morning, Mr. Wright, I'm Lloyd Dickerson from Technical Telephones Inc.," Dickerson was confident and flashed his best prospecting smile. "I came by this morning to talk with you about your telephone system. I'd like only about five minutes of your time, sir, if I may?"

Another one of these young telephone hot shots, Bill Wright thought with an internal sigh. *Oh well, why not let him talk. It shouldn't take long to discourage this one.*

"Okay, son, shoot. What's on your mind?" he said.

"Well, I'd like to ask you a few questions first, if I may?"

"Whatever you like. But I should tell you right up front that I'm not really in the market for a new phone system."

"Well, perhaps that's because you haven't had a chance to see what Technical Telephones can do for you. I couldn't help noticing when I came in that you have a very old South Electric Telephone switchboard in your front office. How old is it exactly?"

"It's a 1958 antique. Isn't it a beauty?"

"Did you buy it new?" Lloyd asked, thinking, *He's got to be kidding. That old thing should have been trashed twenty years ago.*

"Yeah . . . well . . . I didn't exactly. It was my dad who made the choice. It's done us proud ever since."

"Uh-huh. Uh, . . . who did you buy it from?"

"Actually from the South Electric Telephone Company itself."

"Gee, are they still in business?"

"Oh, I don't know. We have never had any need to call them so . . . I don't really . . ."

"I see. Well, it's obviously pretty old now and I'm sure it can't really still handle the demands of a growing and dynamic business like yours is today. Have you ever seen the Technical Telephone model X95 switchboard?"

"Uh . . . a fella was in here just about six months ago, wanted me to look at something that sounded like that. I can't be sure though."

"Oh? Do you recall his name?"

"Sure. It was Bass. I remember because I love to fish and bass is my favorite catch. So naturally I remembered his name."

"I don't think we had anyone working for us by that name six months ago. Could he have been with another phone company?"

"Oh, he might have been. I couldn't say. It's just that his name caught my fancy is all."

"Ah! Okay . . . uh . . . where was I?"

"Asking me if I'd ever seen one of your top-of-the-line models, I believe."

"Yes! Yes! I wanted to show you this brochure that points out how it handles up to twenty-one incoming calls simultaneously and frees your receptionist from the need to pull plugs and replug them like she's doing now. It can even record messages or forward calls to you if you are in another office, or to someone you designate to answer for you when you don't want to handle calls yourself.

"You see this little button right here on the lower-left control panel?" Lloyd slipped around the side of Wright's desk to join him so he could show him the picture. This was a trick he'd learned years ago for getting himself over on the prospect's side of the desk. It was a lot harder to say no to someone standing beside you.

"That little button is the master control switch. Once you've programmed the system, you just touch that button to activate any feature you want. That's some piece of work, isn't it?"

Wright was appalled by Dickerson's coming in behind his desk. *The nerve of the guy!* he thought. *Well, that was it, then. Time to close up shop on this one!*

"Look son, I know you've got a living to make, and that you've got to sell phone systems to do it, but understand, loud and clear, I'm not in the market for one. I won't be in the market for one now or in the future. If I ever change my mind, I may give you a call. Leave your card and any literature you want with my secretary on your way out. And please don't bother to call again!"

A not untypical response to a somewhat typical sales approach.

What went wrong? Why couldn't Dickerson get to first base?

The consultative seller will say it's because Dickerson concentrated on his product and not on partnering the prospect. The systematic seller will feel that it is because he had no system, that he knew nothing about the prospect's needs and simply threw a scattershot sales pitch at him rather than presenting a system tailored to his needs. The needs satisfaction seller would agree and add that poor Dickerson didn't use the right probes, that he used too many closed-ended ones to really uncover the prospect's needs. And the conceptual seller would insist that Dickerson lost the prospect because he was selling his product rather than selling the prospect on what that product could do for him, the concept of a modern telephone system.

All of them would be partially right. Each of these shortcomings did influence the outcome of the interview. But none of them was the root cause of the failure. The problem was that Mr. Wright simply *was not ready to buy* a telephone system. He was a poor prospect. The fact that he had an antiquated system made absolutely no difference. He did not see it as antiquated. He was happy with its performance. He was plainly not yet ready even to look at a new one. Trying to sell a telephone system to someone in that frame of mind is, and always will be, a complete waste of time.

When do you buy a new car? Can a sales agent sell you one before you are ready to buy one? Perhaps you might consider buying a car if the agent was giving it away at a price so low that even other dealers flocked in to buy it. But even then you'd probably have to ask yourself what you would do with another car. How about a house? Can a real estate agent sell you a new house when you are not in the market, when you have just moved into your dream house? Of course not.

Yet, as salespeople, we follow the myth that we can sell anything to anyone if only we are good enough. When we fail, we excuse ourselves by saying something like, "Oh well, you can't sell refrigerators to Eskimos." Actually, Eskimos do buy refrigerators—when they are in the market for them! An Eskimo in an igloo has no need of artificial refrigeration. But an Eskimo in a settlement, working for an oil company or on a construction crew, definitely needs one, knows it, and can be sold one by any proficient salesperson. "Of course," you say, "that's obvious!" And yet we persist in the myth that we can *sell* something to others. The fact is, however, that if the customer doesn't want the product, "selling" won't make him or her buy it. Coercion might, but "selling" never will!

It is a simple but hard truth that if the prospect doesn't want what the salesperson has to offer there will be no sale. Every con artist knows this. P. T. Barnum built his empire on it. Race track touts thrive on it. Telemarketing boiler rooms, gambling casinos, state lotteries, and politicians all practice it every day. Yet salespeople continue to ignore it, continue to "push for the sale," to make elaborate "sales pitches," to "close aggressively," and to wonder why selling is such a difficult job! They fail to realize that so long as they persist in ignoring the fact that people are not sold, but buy only when they are ready, it will continue to seem to be a difficult job.

The problem lies in the fact that most sales training and sales literature is focused on the salesperson's activity in "selling" and not on the buyer's reactions. Little mention is made of selling objectives except as dollar goals or prospecting numbers that the salesperson must achieve to be successful. Yet the sale depends more on a set of reactions *on the part of the buyer* than it does on the actions of the seller.

This is plain common sense. Yet, as a sales trainer, I am continually surprised when even experienced and successful salespeople are unable to frame a sales call objective describing the *prospect's* reaction rather than what the *salesperson* plans to say or do. It isn't their fault. It's how they have been trained. People naturally think of what they are going to do, or say, or accomplish. It's hard to take on the external perspective of an unbiased observer and ask, "So what effect will this behavior of mine have on the other person? Is that the reaction I want? What reaction do I really want?"

The answer to this last question is called a *behavioral* objective, which differs from the usual self-descriptive sales objective in that it describes not what the seller aims at doing but rather what the buyer's reaction will be to the seller's behavior. After all, the purpose of making a sales contact is to have the buyer buy. The buyer/seller relationship needs to be defined in terms of results, not selling activities.

Like any action to which one may aspire, such a set of reactions can be described in terms of behavioral objectives. Unfortunately, most of the literature on selling is oriented mainly toward the salesperson's reactions, goals, or purposes. Buyer "needs" are dealt with as though they were some sort of hidden treasure that the salesperson must discover in order to "close" the sale.

This book is a response to what seems to be a clearly apparent need. It is an approach to selling that concentrates on how to plan sales efforts to coincide with the buyer's wants, to take advantage of the customer's interest and readiness to buy. It breaks with the traditional approach, which fosters the impossible-to-fulfill ideal that a good salesperson can force a sale on an unwilling buyer by using "good" sales techniques.

The topics covered in these chapters do not differ greatly from the topics usually covered in a sales book: prospecting, presenting, controlling the sale, handling objections, understanding needs, closing, and so forth. What is radically different is the perspective from which each of these topics is examined. Prospecting, for instance, ceases to be an endless series of knocked-upon doors and becomes a modern marketing tool for zeroing in on only those prospects who are most likely to be ready to buy. Probing, that most unfortunate word, becomes a study in the responses to suspicion and lack of trust on the part of the prospect. It is also a series of techniques for controlling such fears and building the trust that is integral to the buying process.

In the course of these ten chapters, every step of selling is examined from the point of view of the contribution it makes to the behavioral objective of the sales call. The result of such a call is never what the salesperson does or even wants to do. It is, instead, what the potential buyer does in response to what that salesperson has done.

This perspective did not come to me in a flash of inspiration. Rather, it has grown and been refined over fifteen years of a very successful career in selling and in managing salespeople, and in the course of twelve years of training salespeople and their managers in public seminars, private in-house workshops, and one-on-one coaching sessions covering a broad range of industries and organizations. Consequently, I frequently draw on both my sales seminars and my own direct selling experience to illustrate various points. Salespeople should feel free to identify with the situations as I describe them, for all of them are true, all of them have happened, just as they are reported here, and, so, all of them are opportunities for examining my approach to selling in action.

Because it reflects an approach to selling that has helped thousands, this book is intended to serve as a reference for the full spectrum of selling. It can be used by newly hired potential salespeople to direct their skills acquisition so that they can begin their careers soundly and several jumps ahead of the competition. So, if you are new to selling, follow the tenets set out here and you will find that not only will you begin to sell more sooner, but you will feel very comfortable doing so. On the other hand, if you are a seasoned professional, the book is designed so that by following its tenets, you will be able to increase your closing averages and, perhaps more important, build a loyal customer base for repeat business. If you are a follower of any of the sales schools I have referred to earlier, no matter how you were originally trained to sell, reexamine the system you learned in the light of what is said here and you will be able to fine tune and personalize your skills even more. If you learned selling in the school of hard knocks, you'll find that this book explains many of the phenomena you've observed over the years and it will help you to sharpen your responses to customers and to better understand the processes taking place while you are selling. And if you are a sales manager or a trainer of salespeople, I can promise you that working through the contents of this book with your people will help you and them to diagnose problems and develop needed skills effectively. This book is for all who sell and who want to continue to grow and develop their professional selling skills.

One final word before we launch our journey through the principles of customer-oriented selling: I have used several conventions in writing this book that you should be aware of. As every customer is also a prospect for further sales, and every prospect is potentially a customer, I use the terms more or less interchangeably. When it is important to draw a distinction between them, I let you know that I am doing so. Otherwise, I alternate between them for the sake of variety rather than as a distinction of meaning. I also alternate between the singular and plural in discussing prospects or salespeople and between "he" and "she" when giving individual examples.

By now you are no doubt impatient to begin so let's turn to Chapter 1 and discover how marketing differs from prospecting and how you can capitalize on that difference.

1

Marketing vs. Prospecting

As you sit reading this book, stop a moment and look around you. When your eye falls upon something you've bought that you originally saw advertised on television or in print ads, ask yourself, "How did the producers of that article manage to find the right place to advertise it so that I would buy it? How did they find the right potential market? How do the folks who send me direct-mail advertising know that I might be a prospective buyer?"

Perhaps you're thinking the answer is mailing lists. But then ask yourself, how they happened to pick the particular list with your name on it from among the hundreds of thousands of mailing lists they have access to at any given time.

The fact is that they know you will be a potential buyer before they ever create the advertisement that they will use to sell their wares to you.

How Does Kellogg's Sell Corn Flakes?

Kellogg's and other successful companies use *marketing* rather than *prospecting* to find their customers. These are two quite different approaches. Prospecting is like fishing in unknown waters. You know you have to go out on the water in your boat and throw out a line as often as you can. You hope you might get lucky and catch a fish that happens by chance to be both hungry and looking at your lure when you cast it. You have no idea how big the fish will be, what kind of fish it will be, what the right time to try to lure it is or even what kind of lure you should be using. You just cast and cast on the theory that fishing is a numbers game and that if you cast often enough you're bound to get a nibble eventually.

Marketing, on the other hand, is more like fishing in a stocked lake or where the schools of fish are running, at predictable feeding times, for a known species that has always responded to the lure you have created to catch it. "Ah," you say, "but that's not as sporting." You're quite right. And neither is selling! It is a business, just as marketing is a business, and your task, as with all business ventures, should be to produce the maximum results with the minimum effort. Marketing does so extremely well. Prospecting succeeds only occasionally and by chance.

"So how does marketing accomplish this remarkable efficiency?" you ask. It works generally like this. When a product like Corn Flakes is to be introduced and put on the market, the creative people at the advertising agency meet in order to decide what sort of person will buy such a product. They describe the physical attributes, emotional states, social habits, income levels, eating patterns, sex, age, and, if need be, political affiliation of the ideal potential user of the product. The art department will even draw pictures of what this person looks like. They will decide what colors the prospect likes, what flavors, how he or she will dress, what car they will drive, and where they will live. And they will do all this without ever seeing or going out to meet anyone in the real world who might want to eat a bowl of this nutritious cereal.

Once they think they know precisely who their prospects are, they hold a series of what are called focus groups. They invite a number of different kinds of average consumers to sit around a table for an hour or two to taste the cereal and to discuss what they think of it. While these folks are eating and talking, the creative teams study them carefully for their reactions, their likes and dislikes, and mostly, to verify that the imaginary target person they have created is on track. The eventual advertisement will be directed at this ideal target, and the folks who will create that ad want to be sure that he or she will be the right prospect for their campaign.

While the creative groups are formulating the ideal target for the ad campaign, and clarifying the unique attributes of the product that will help to sell it, the marketing department of the advertising agency is carefully defining how big a market the ad campaign will try to address. They are fully aware of the pitfalls of overmarketing. If the ad campaign is so successful that it produces more orders than the company can fill, it becomes self-defeating and produces bad will instead of happy customers. On the other hand, if the target market is too small, the company won't be getting the maximum return for its advertising dollar, and that costs the advertising agency future business.

In effect, then, while the creative groups are defining the ideal customer, the marketing groups work to refine the size and scope of the overall target market. They set the sales goals that will eventually measure the success (or failure) of the ad campaign.

Once they know who their customer is and how many such customers they want to reach, they can at last look at the real world to discover where the desired number of the right customers are. This is the stage in which mailing lists are examined, television ratings and print circulation demographics are studied and compared to the pre-set specifications the ad teams have devised. Now they can look at what the competition is doing in the marketplace and decide on the market segment their flakes will have to go after and how large a share of that segment they will need to target.

Finally, out of this step, the test market area will emerge. A section of the country or the population will be carved out for a trial run. The actual advertising messages will at last be written and produced and the product will be made available to the select public that has been demographically segregated. The results will be analyzed and if they are as good as they were predicted to be the agency will "roll out" the full nationwide campaign.

Essentially what has happened here is that the mass marketing experts have devised a way to make their work much more efficient by approaching only those prospects who are likely to buy whatever it is they are selling. The rest of the public they leave alone. They don't do this by laboriously feeling their way in the dark, as most traditional prospectors do. Instead, they zero in on the prospects who want to buy now without wasting time or money or effort on those who will resist.

The Five Steps to Marketing in Sales

Of course the pattern we've just discussed is a general one. Different products may demand different treatment, or an advertising agency may try to make its mark by breaking the rules. However, the general pattern holds true for most advertised products. And it works. Furthermore, it illustrates exactly my point in this book: Selling is much more efficient when the prospects approached are limited to those who are most likely to buy.

There are five separate steps to the process. Whereas the advertising world has the luxury of separate divisions (marketing, creative, and account or client contact) to handle different steps, the individual salesperson must handle each alone.

For the rest of this chapter, we will look at each step in turn. Because it is a more complex process, we will cover Step Three, researching sources, further and in much greater depth in Chapter 2. Similarly, qualifying your prospects, reaching them by mail and by telephone, will be covered in detail in Chapter 3. The rest of the book, chapters 4 through 10, is devoted to Step Five, calling on your prospects and presenting them with the opportunity to buy from you.

Specify What You're Selling and Who'll Buy It

One of the major differences between the marketing approach to selling and the traditional sales approach is in where planning begins. For traditional sellers it starts just before the sales call. For the marketer, it starts much earlier with defining exactly what is to be sold and who is likely to buy it. This is the first new habit you will have to adopt in order to take advantage of the unique principles in this book. We start by carefully defining the product or service you will be selling.

Most of us know what we are selling. In fact, the most common form of sales training throughout the world is in product knowledge. Yet specifying what you are selling goes beyond mere physical characteristics. It goes beyond listing the features or the competitive advantages your product or service responds to in the marketplace. It even goes beyond the benefits that customers will enjoy once they have purchased from you. It includes these, of course, but it must also spell out the concept, the idea, the system and the relationship of the product or service to other elements within that system. Miller and Meiman's "conceptual selling" works here. But it is here at this early planning stage that it works, not face to face with the prospect. Of course conceptual selling has a profound impact on the relationship between the seller and the prospect, but that impact can be dramatically increased if the planning, if the specifying, if this prime step to effective marketing in sales is carefully addressed first.

Five Steps to Marketing in Sales

1. Specify precisely what it is that you are selling and exactly who is most likely to want to buy it.
2. Decide how many new customers you can afford to service and exactly when you need to have them.
3. Research sources to identify and find these newly defined prospects.
4. Qualify these prospects to narrow the market to a usable size, determine their buying cycle, and discover the position of the competition.
5. Call on them to offer the opportunity to buy from you.

Once you have a clear idea of precisely what it is that you are selling, and how it fits in the marketplace, you must decide who will buy it, who will be the best possible prospects to approach. At this point in my sales seminars I ask the attendees to list briefly the characteristics that describe their ideal customer. As "ideal customers" vary from individual to individual and product to product, the answers I get range from high pie-in-the-sky fantasies (for example, someone who needs my product or service desperately, has cash in hand, knows of absolutely no other supplier, and who is extremely grateful that I came along to help out) to touching revelations of the struggles involved in doing business (my favorite is a poor fellow who said that his ideal customer was anyone who wouldn't give him too much trouble!). Both of these extremes, by the way, are legitimate descriptions of an ideal customer. Such factors are, however, usually very hard to identify in the marketplace. Still, it doesn't hurt to define them and then to consciously look for them.

Within the range suggested by these two extremes, however, some very accessible information emerges. It falls into two classifications—commercially available demographics and personal, private, inside information. Into the first category fall such things as past purchasing patterns, income levels, size of organization, managers' names and phone numbers, market conditions, and so forth. We'll be dealing in detail with the sources for this kind of information in the next chapter.

The second category is usually much more difficult to come by. It consists of information on such things as how the prospect bargains, what the internal political situation is in the prospect's personal life or company, or exactly what the prospect needs and when. These sources will be covered in detail in the next chapter, too, but at this point I only want you to think about the fact that there is a body of information available to each of you that is seldom tapped and yet can help you considerably to find those prospects who are most likely to buy from you.

In fact, put this book aside for a moment. Take up a piece of paper and a pencil, and describe your ideal customer. Start with a description of the three best customers you have right now. Who are they? How often do they buy from you? What closed the sale to them for you? Why don't they give you "too much trouble?" What are their needs? When will they have them? What can they afford to spend? When will they (or you) know? What, exactly, makes them your "best" customers? Be hard on yourself here. Don't give glib, superficial answers. Think about it. Hard. The more accurately you can describe them, the better you will be able to target just the right prospects in the future.

When you have a list of defining characteristics, put it aside until you get to Chapter 2. There we will look at sources of information that will give you a chance to verify the impressions you've just written down; or to enhance them with new information; or to redefine in higher relief your relationship to your current customers. The sheet of paper you have now is a working draft of the description you will eventually create of your ideal prospective customer.

How Many New Customers Do You Want, and When?

Time after time salespeople tell me "I want all the customers I can get! I want every last person or company that I can lay my hands on for a customer!" Many salespeople seem to think that such a state of affairs would be paradise. It wouldn't. There is a species of frog in which the male cannot tell the difference between other males and females of its own kind. During the mating season, the male frog simply leaps onto anything that moves. If it accepts him, fine. If not—no problem. Either way, he just jumps onto the next one he sees. If you act like that frog and jump onto everything that moves to try to sell it something, your whole attention will be devoted to the *next* prospect, invariably at the expense of the current one. You can sell, but you have no time or interest in servicing those you've already sold. You become the stereotypical, "buyer beware," pushy salesman (unfortunately it is a male stereotype), and your reputation spreads to the point where you meet nothing but resistance.

Furthermore, no company can survive for long selling

more customers than it can satisfy. How do you feel when you arrive at a store to buy something and find that it is sold out? That there is a back order list three miles long and that it will be at least eight weeks before your order can be processed? Not too pleased, I'll bet.

A client of mine, a telemarketing firm, was recently engaged to conduct a nationwide canvasing program for a company that was anxious to expand rapidly. Working together, my client and I created a campaign for the company that succeeded in generating thousands of hot leads, prospects truly anxious to buy this particular new service. Unfortunately, the company was simply not large enough nor sufficiently geared up to respond appropriately to the volume of leads we generated. It couldn't hire and train staff fast enough to handle the demand it had created. As a result, it went out of business in a snowstorm of lawsuits initiated by a lot of miserable, unhappy folk who had truly been ready to buy, had wanted the service, and who were now bitterly disappointed and even cynical about anyone else who might try to sell them something. What a terrible and unnecessary waste!

With no objective to focus on, progress is unlikely. By setting clearly defined target goals you can plan, monitor, and direct your own sales success. If you are a commissioned sales representative, the most effective way to begin is by considering the following series of questions and procedures for yourself:

1. How much money do you want to be making twelve months from now?
2. How many sales must you make in order to earn that amount?
3. Can you handle and service that number of customers? If not, how many can you handle?
4. How many of this number will come to you in the normal course of business (through walk-ins, corporate leads, unsolicited referrals, responses to national advertising, repeat business, and so forth)? Subtract this number from the number desired. The total will be the number of new customers you must generate to

earn your desired income. These you will have to find on your own.

5. Based on your current closing average, how many new prospects will you have to call on in order to gain this new business? This is the number of new prospects you must find and contact.

6. Can you accomplish this in less time than a year? Will it take longer than a year? This step sets your time goal.

Of course, if you are self-employed or work on a salary basis in which commissions don't influence your income, you might have to use some other figure base in steps one and two. Perhaps volume of sales would work for you. In either case, whether you work on salary or on commission, the answers to these questions will set your goals for you. This step, coupled with the definition of your ideal customer and what you are selling, is the most essential guide to effective customer-oriented selling. All of your prospecting research and follow-up qualifying will be influenced by your answers to this set of six questions.

Research Sources for Finding These New Prospects

Once you have defined what you're selling, who you are selling it to, how many new prospects you'll need, and the time frame for acquiring them, you can begin to look for them in the real world. As we shall see in the next chapter, there are many sources of commercially available demographic information. The inside, personal information is much harder to come by, but we will look at a number of sources and approaches you can adapt to your sales market in Chapter 2 as well.

It is important to note here, however, that this is an essential step, not one to be glossed over. To say, "Oh, I know all that stuff, I'm just gonna go out there and sell," is self-defeating. If you fail to spend the time looking for and building up the sources that tell you when the prospects are ready to buy and most likely, therefore, to be sellable, then you are simply repeating the 1970s selling procedure this book is designed to help you to move away from. Customers *do* buy when they are ready. Effective selling in the 1990s is a matter of calling on them and presenting them with your offer of help when they need it, not when they are not interested. Armed with the definitions and goals we've already discussed, following this research step allows you to do just that. Failing to do this research makes the rest of the process we'll be discussing a waste of time. This step is crucial!

Qualify the Prospects From the Source Material

It would be nice to have a world so precise that once we had found a prospect on a list of likely ones we could be assured that this prospect would definitely be in the market for our product or service. Unfortunately, mass marketing is not an exact science. Your research will turn up prospects that are most likely to be in the market. But there are no guarantees. So most of them will still have to be qualified.

By using the commercial source material detailed in this book you will probably come up with far more names than you could ever want or need. You will have to break down the lists into smaller, more manageable chunks. There are several ways to do this.

First, set up a cross-reference system. Take a list of names that has been selected according to one of your ideal customer criteria, then select from it only those names that match another, different criterion. This process can be repeated again and again until you have on your list only that number of names you feel you can handle. And for each of those names you will have a number of matched criteria that indicate that this prospect will buy now. The more criteria you can match, the better the likelihood that the prospects are ready.

A simpler but consequently broader stroked system would be to narrow down the list geographically. Of course such an approach has nothing to do with the prospect's likelihood of buying, but it does help you to qualify on the basis of time and travel efficiency. Place yourself at the center of a circle on a map. Make the radius of the circle (the distance from you at the center to any place on the outer rim) a reasonable physical distance for you and the area you have to cover. Then, any names from your list that fall inside the circle are good prospects merely because they are close by and easy to service. All of those that fall outside the circle can be put on the back burner to be called on when, and if, you manage to sell all of those inside the circle.

A third alternative would be to select them by their product or buying life cycles. Every product goes through a life cycle. It starts on a drawing board, goes through a design and prototype stage, then is tested, and if it works it is marketed to its potential buyers. Eventually the sales volume will peak and begin to decline and, unless some innovation or new packaging is created to rekindle the market, it will drift into a decline and finally be superseded by something new.

As customers we tend to go through much the same cycle. We start slow with a "show me" attitude, become convinced, buy, enjoy, and then begin to accept what we've bought as "old hat," so that either some new wrinkle must restimulate us or we will look afield for another, newer product or service. Most individuals live through a lifelong buying cycle as well. As children we buy little (parents make the big money decisions). Once out of school, we can make our own decisions, but few of us have the money to be able to buy much. Finally, we make enough money, set up our own homes and families, succeed at work, and become prime consumers. Eventually, however, our kids grow up and move away, we spend less, retire, and buy less and less until we need to be cared for by someone else who makes the buying decisions again.

In the case of business customers, it is pointless to sell at the prototype stage if you want immediate results. If you want to lock in your service or product for the later success stage, then this is a good time to sell, but expect the results to pay off years down the road. Ideally, the best time to sell is during the early roll-out time so that as your customer grows into full production so does that customer's business with you.

The best time to sell to individuals who are happy with the product or service they are using is in the "getting tired of it" stage, when they begin to look around at alternatives. The automotive industry excels at this. Demographically, domestic car owners tend to sell their cars after twenty-four to twenty-eight months. Foreign car owners sell theirs after about thirty-six months. These are therefore the prime target times in the selling cycle for car sales personnel to approach customers. This is when you will receive literature from car manufacturers after you have bought one of their new cars. And nearly all the auto manufacturers are now offering telephone prospecting skills training to their salespeople.

Finally, most consumers are likely to have the money, the inclination, and the need from ages 30 through 55 or so. These are the prime buying years. Obviously particular professions or regions of the country will cause such broad demographics to vary considerably, but giving consideration to them is one of the swiftest and easiest ways to chunk the vast numbers of potential prospects down to a handleable size.

A final consideration for qualifying the lists of prospects down to size is the activity of your own competition. It is always easier to sell around them than it is to confront them one on one. Look for the prospects who don't use or like the competition and narrow your lists down to them. Or, by asking your current customers or prospects, find out where your competitors are sending in their best salespeople and sell elsewhere.

In all cases, what you are doing in this step is "creaming the list." This is a term from direct marketing that I will be using frequently throughout the early parts of this book; it refers to the practice of selecting only the very best prospects (the cream) from a list and selling only to them. Direct mailers know that one percent or less of the people to whom they send mailings will actually buy from them. They know that the 99 percent of those who do not buy regard the mailing as "junk mail" to be thrown away instantly. They also know that they cannot really sell a new product or idea with a simple advertising letter. What they are looking for is that one percent who are already interested, who are ready to buy, who recognize that they need whatever it is that is being offered and so can be easily sold. This is the direct mailer's or the telephone seller's market. They don't expect or even want those who don't buy to respond. They are "creaming the list" to interest only the ones who already want to buy from them. What you need to do is to adapt the same approach to face-to-face selling.

Call on Them to Offer the Opportunity to Buy

The last of the five steps is the traditional sales call. I will devote a considerable portion of this book to discussing ways to enhance it and to control and shape it in ways that are untraditional but highly effective in the modern marketplace. Here I would like only to put it into its proper perspective. It is a part of a whole marketing cycle.

We in sales have been brought up to concentrate on this phase alone and to neglect or to remain ignorant of the preceding four steps. After all, our company does market research for us, doesn't it? Why should we get involved in their job? The answer is simple: because selling to people who already want to buy is a great deal easier than trying to sell to those who don't. The first four steps we've been looking at here together constitute the best way for you to ensure that this is what you are doing when you take step five and go out to make a sales call.

Remember the distinction with which we began this chapter: that traditional approaches to prospecting are rather like fly-fishing—difficult, time-consuming, requiring a great deal of luck, but sometimes quite successful; whereas marketing is closer to fishing in a stocked lake at known feeding times, where failure is the rarity, not success. In sales, the crucial difference between the two lies in two areas: first, in the amount of time devoted to planning, the type of research conducted, and when that planning and research are begun; and second, in a shift toward awareness of customer needs, desires, and responses and away from the traditional focus on making the sale. The next two chapters will help you to accomplish the first, and the rest of the book will help you to master the second. Together, these skills will allow you to become an even more effective, truly customer-oriented salesperson.

You have enough information at least to start on this new

program right now. But many people feel unfamiliar with the world of research and quite a few salespeople I talk to are not as effective on the telephone as they could be, so before we leave prospecting we're going to take a couple of chapters to examine each of these two crucial skills.

2

How to Market Rather Than Prospect

After reading Chapter 1 and working up a precise description of your ideal customer, you are probably sitting back and saying to yourself, "Yup! That's the one alright! That's the best prospect for me. But now what? How am I supposed to find all of the people out there who match this description? Where do I look?" That's what we're going to cover in this chapter.

The first question you must ask yourself when you begin to market rather than prospect is, "What do I need to know about a potential prospect in order for that company or person to become a genuine sales lead?" If your goal is to capitalize on the customer's desire to buy, and that is indeed the premise of this book, then knowing when customers have that desire is paramount. The single most important bit of information you can gather, therefore, is simply the knowledge of when they are ready to buy. All other information is secondary. Of course you need to know who to call on and where to find them, but such facts are only useful when you first know when they will need whatever it is that you are selling. This is the beginning of the marketing process, so efficient prospecting becomes a matter of using a marketing approach to finding sources of information that will reveal the prospect's buying cycle.

Sources of Prospecting Information

There are actually so many sources of potential prospecting information that the sheer number of them can become a major problem. How do you select which ones are best for you, your industry, your product or service? I recommend that you pick four, or at the most five, sources and then concentrate on them. You might be happy with only the minimum one or two, but you should limit yourself to no more than four or five, tops. The problem is simply one of inundation. Marketers need to produce large numbers of target buyers; salespeople need comparatively fewer numbers of good prospects. No one wants to have to call on 5,000 new prospects. If you have that many, you will have to spend a great deal of time honing that list down to only 500 or so. The governing factor becomes the number of new prospects you want to sell to, in other words, how many new customers you feel you can handle in a specific time frame, which you decided on in the last chapter.

Different sources will yield different numbers and different levels of specific information. A commercial mailing list, no matter how specialized, is designed to include thousands of names, each qualified only in a limited way. On the other hand, a personal lead-swapping network will generate only a few high-quality leads each month. If you follow the cross-referencing system I suggested in Chapter 1, you will need at least two sources and perhaps three or more in order to use each to narrow down the selections of the others.

There are many ways to list and explain the various sources for prospecting names and buying-cycle information. Many of the sources are common both to business-to-business selling and to direct consumer sales. Some sources are free and others can be quite costly. All require some degree of effort and time on your part. The free sources tend to require the largest investment of your time, whereas vendor-prepared sources tend to be more expensive. The best place to start is with sources that are commonly available to all salespeople.

A small explanation is in order before we do, however. Many salespeople feel that there is a large and very important difference between selling a service and selling a product, so wherever possible I will underline the distinctions when they apply. But in market research—in seeking sources of lists of qualified prospects to call on—whether you sell a product or a service will make no appreciable difference in where you look for names. Whether you sell business to business or directly to consumers is a much more important distinction in list selection.

Personal Sources

The single best source of the most potent sales leads is other salespeople. Everyone who sells has had the experience of getting a great lead from a friend or fellow sales rep that turned out to be a terrific customer.

Consider the following situation. I sell tailor-made sales training seminars. One of my colleagues sells high-risk specialty insurance. While I am calling on one of my long-term best customers, he (the customer) vents his dissatisfaction and concern over the high cost of insurance. He knows I'm not in the insurance business and can do nothing for him, but he's frustrated, it's on his mind, and I'm a good listener. However, seeing that he has a problem, I say something like, "You know, Bill, I have a colleague who specializes in personally tailored insurance for businesses like yours. I'd like to give her your name and ask her to call on you. I think she could help a lot with the situation. Would you mind if I asked her to give you a call?" If he wants a solution to his problem, and usually he does, he'll say, "No. Ask her to call!"

When my colleague walks in the door to Bill's office, she has several things going for her. First, she has all the years of credibility I have built up with this client going for her. She still needs to make a good impression, right enough, but it is only to fulfill Bill's expectations rather than to create a new relationship starting from scratch. Second, she knows Bill wants to buy. He has a problem and he *expects* her to solve it for him. She knows she is calling at the right time to capitalize on Bill's desire to buy. Third, she has no competition. As yet, Bill hasn't gone into the marketplace to look for a solution. Instead, he has asked for her personal service in this instance. Folks, this is a dream sale because the hard part of selling is already taken care of; only the buying part remains.

"Well, but that's only hypothetical," you say. "Those kinds of leads don't just happen like that. If they did I'd be rich!" And you'd be right. They don't really just happen. They require an organized system of regular lead swapping, a consciously maintained network of key sales professionals, and the habit of keeping your eyes open for opportunities outside your own selling field. And when you do all of this, such things *do* happen, regularly. And, yes, you would be rich if you had built and maintained your personal sales lead network. I've had salespeople say to me, "Boy, if I could get one or two of those a month, I'd be rich!" Well, you can have them. Even three, four, or five of them per month if you like. But you have to work for them. They won't drop off the trees into your lap.

So, in order to create a steady flow of high-quality leads, you must build a lead-swapping network. Seek out parallel, noncompetitive salespeople, people who sell to the same customers you sell to but who sell something that doesn't compete with your service or product line. Don't limit yourself to just salespeople, either. Many professionals whom we don't traditionally think of as salespeople must sell their services all the same. Lawyers, architects, consultants, retail store managers, bankers, and contractors all have to generate new business and sell their services and products, often to the same people you sell to. Spend a few minutes mulling over who besides yourself might also be calling on your customers. Put this book aside for five minutes, right now, and make up a list of the vendors with whom your customers deal every day. This is your starting point.

Some people say to me, "I don't know what else my customers buy. How do you expect me to know that, for goodness sake?" Ask your customers. Look around you when you visit them. Ask their employees or neighbors. You'll be surprised at how happy they will be to tell you. Say to your best customer, "Aside from myself, who are the two or three best salespeople who call on you?" They'll be pleased to tell you. Go to the purchasing agent in your own company (or to members of your family if you sell directly to consumers) and say, "Who are the two or three really good salespeople that you like to deal with?" They'll let you know. Call up any of those noncompetitive vendors on your list, ask to talk to the sales manager, and say "I'm interested in setting up a lead-swapping arrangement with your two best salespeople. Could we set up a meeting to get something like that going?" I don't know of a sales manager alive who'd turn you down.

If you travel when you sell, why waste lonely evenings in your hotel room watching TV? Many hotels have "travelers' tables" in their restaurants where those who'd like to can meet, talk, and exchange business information over dinner. If the hotels you stay in don't have one, take a table for five or six, if you can, and ask the maitre d' or the hostess, if he or she would ask those who come in alone if they would care to join you (or your group once a few take you up on the offer). Some of the pleasantest evenings I have ever spent on the road have been passed this way. And the leads I've garnered have been first-rate. I realize that there is an element of risk in such an approach, particularly if you are a woman traveling alone. There are men who would attempt to take sexual advantage of the situation rather than use it to further business. This is why I suggest that you do it through the hotel, not on your own. And, of course, some hotels lend themselves to such events much more readily than others. Use your discretion.

Once you make contact with someone for lead swapping, set up a regular meeting schedule. I recommend a meeting every two weeks or even once a month. Many groups meet weekly, but I find that when that happens the quality of the leads goes downhill. People feel too pressured to get leads and so crank out easy ones that are not well qualified. The purpose here is not to generate lots of leads. It is, rather, to generate a few high-quality leads. It is, after all, the quality of the leads that makes the meetings worthwhile.

Limit the size of your group as well. There are many excellent service organizations that traditionally foster networking. They are fine, but usually much too large. The quality leads I'm talking about here require a smaller group whose members actively seek business for each other and who meet solely for the purpose of swapping leads. I'd suggest no more than ten members at the most. Such a group could be a subset of a larger service organization or it could be a totally different group of people. Members can be friends, but they needn't be. The purpose is business pure and simple. Socialize later, if you'd like, but keep the meetings about business. Breakfast meetings are often very profitable because they tend to be shorter, more businesslike, and can start the day off with a bang.

A second easily accessible free source of information on buying cycles and good prospects is your company's records. Depending on what you sell, your company will keep records on such things as services performed, customer service responses, complaints, current orders, past orders, and so on. All of these are capable of generating new prospects, or at least of regenerating old ones.

One type of record that has generated a number of excellent successful sales for me over the years is old sales call or trade show contact reports. You can examine your own or someone else's. Don't pore over each one, but thumb quickly through the pile looking only for those that are marked as "good potential" or "interested" prospects, yet nobody got around to following up on them. Or, if they were contacted, the timing was off, they weren't ready then, or they were unavailable and no one ever got back to them. Call them up to see if it's time yet. I cannot count the number of sales I've made with this simple technique. I've found that once prospects are interested, they usually remain interested.

All too often we tend to feel discouraged by a lack of interest on the part of a prospect. We dismiss such uninterested folk as "uninformed" or "too pigheaded to know what's good for them," or we feel simply that "they don't like me, so

I won't deal with them." We feel down, personally rejected and defeated, and therefore never go back to call on them again. What a mistake! These are among the very best prospects we have. Their needs change. Because they didn't realize their need for our product or service today doesn't mean they won't see it tomorrow! We simply called at a time when they were not in the market, were not ready to buy, and so they said "no." But sooner or later, everybody needs to buy. Timing is the point: being there when that need becomes apparent to the prospect. That's when truly successful selling takes place. But the only way to be sure to be there then is to keep on calling back. Persistence sells not when it's pushy and annoying but when it grows out of concern for the prospect's welfare.

There is a business-to-business salesman in New Jersey who tells me that he keeps a Rolodex file of all of the people who don't like him and who refuse to see him when he calls on their companies. Religiously he calls each of them on the telephone every three months. When he is put through, he quietly hangs up the phone because he doesn't want to confront someone who doesn't want to talk to him. What he looks for, and frequently finds, is that the negative person who didn't like him has moved on, changed jobs or companies, and now the salesman has a whole new ballpark to play in. Every business-to-business sales representative can do this. If you sell to consumers, by qualifying them for their buying cycle on the first call you can keep in touch and make this tool work for you as well. Those who do so will make money doing it because they will be there when the situation changes and the prospect recognizes the need to buy.

Everyone knows my third free source for new prospects. We have all been taught to make use of it, yet most of us get lazy and let it slip. I'm talking about referrals. Those of us over fifty will remember the slogan used to advertise Packard cars on the radio and in magazines in the late 1930s and early 1940s: "Ask the man who owns one!" What better resource could we ask for than someone who uses a product or service and likes it? Whenever I have bought an unusual car, people will stop me in parking lots, on the street, or in supermarkets to ask, "How do you like it? Is it a good buy? I'm thinking of getting one; would you recommend it?" They are asking for the input of a total stranger in order to gain some nonsales-oriented, credibile information and assurance that the car they want to buy is a good one. How much more powerful must this pattern be when the person they ask is a trusted and admired friend or colleague? People listen to each other. And if something is good enough for so-and-so, whose judgment I trust, then it must be a good move for me. It is one of the most common forms of justification we have, and every good sales-person should be taking advantage of this facet of human nature by asking for and getting referrals.

The nonbuying folk that surround your prospects are a fourth source of information. You can learn a great deal about the people who do make the buying decision by talking to those who don't. In companies, I always take the time to get to know secretaries, receptionists, elevator operators, floor workers, clerical help, security guards, and other members of the staff. They tell me what's going on in the company, whether or not there is a real need, who else is being called in to present to management, and, most important, what the company's buying cycle and pattern is. They can also tell me who really makes the decisions and who else I should be seeing because although they can't say yes they do have the power to say no.

In the consumer marketplace, regardless of which member of the family you are selling to, talk to the spouse. Talk to the children or other relatives and friends, if possible. They will frequently tell you much more than the one you've actually targeted as your prospect.

From time to time people will say to me, "This seems very manipulative. I'd hate for some sales type to pull that on my family." I would, too, if "some sales type" pulled it on mine. Any of these tools can be abused. If they are by someone trying to sell to you, don't buy from that person. There is, however, a vast difference between "pulling" a technique on some unsuspecting dupe and creating a mutually beneficial relationship around solving a buying decision problem with a customer. This is not just a semantic difference. We will cover the means for establishing that kind of relationship and the motivation for it in chapters 5, 6, and 7. Until you've read them, please take me at my word when I say that, though there are some who will use these tools to take unfair advantage of innocent prospects, I believe that their behavior is wrong, self-defeating, and, worst of all, damaging to the reputations of all salespeople. A sale should always be made for the benefit of *both* the salesperson and the customer.

Public Sources

The personal sources we've been examining so far reveal the best quality, specific personal information. They can indicate clearly when the prospect is ready to buy so that we can plan our sales call for the best possible moment. However, such sources seldom develop sufficient hot leads to keep an ambitious salesperson busy full-time. We must, sooner or later, move to less detailed, less personal sources. These can provide only a reasonable likelihood that the prospect is in the market to buy.

The first of these, excellent for business-to-business sales, is the often-overlooked Yellow Pages. This is the single best source I know for finding the largest plumbing concern in a region or the largest and most successful contractor's supply house. In it you can find professionals of all kinds, restaurants, hospitals, service industries, consumer stores, and so on. In fact, nearly every small to medium-sized business in town will be listed in the Yellow Pages.

"But," you ask, "how will I know when they are ready to buy?" Remember, it costs to have a Yellow Pages entry and therefore only those concerns that are finding it pays for itself will be listed there, and only those that are growing large enough to handle additional business will take out new or larger ad space. Look for the largest ads. Usually this indicates the largest and most successful concern in the field and, therefore, the one most likely to need to buy outside services and products. Compare each new issue of the Yellow Pages with the last one. If an outfit has a new ad or a new entry, it is quite likely enjoying a successful season. With greater success usually comes a greater need for supplies, space, staff, and services.

A second powerful source of prospecting information is the public library. Don't, however, just go to the library hoping you will find something or other that will help you. Instead, use the librarian. Librarians by nature, education, and preference love to give information. Their specialty is both knowing where to find information and knowing how to gather it. Ask to see the reference librarian. If necessary, make an appointment. Show him or her your specification list describing your ideal customer and ask what sources are available to help you. You will be inundated with sources.

In the Appendix to this book I've listed a number of potential sources that the librarian might bring you or guide you to. Among them are two that I recommend you ask for specifically: *Directories in Print* and *The Guide to American Directories*. The latter is generally regarded as the better one, but I've had good luck with both. In either case, you will be amazed at the number and variety of directories of names of people that you will find there. Look for a match between one or more of your specifications and the titles of directories listed. Of course there is no way you can be certain that the folks whose names are listed in one of the directories you will find referenced in either of these books will be ready to buy, but, by drawing your specifications carefully, you can increase the likelihood considerably.

The third public source I recommend that you try is your local and state government. The town, or county, or parish clerk's office is frequently a gold mine of free information. This is particularly true for those of you who sell direct to consumers. The public clerk's office records such useful demographics as all of the new businesses in town, real estate transactions, building permits and waivers, apartment and house leases, automobiles purchased, births, deaths, marriages, tax rates and delinquencies, property values, family size, and so forth. If your market is new young families, do-it-yourselfers, successful entrepreneurs, new home owners, people in large houses, or a host of other possible targets, you'll find those who are currently active or are about to be so in the near future. Sell to them, for they are likely to be ready to buy.

The state government usually has a collection of excellent directories for business-to-business sales that list company names and locations, size and volume of business, number of employees, and so forth. If these and similar facts are your demographics, you will find the state an excellent source. You should contact the department of commerce or the department of economic development as the most likely to be helpful with business sources. Depending on the data you need, however, other potentially helpful sources are the departments of air pollution, banking, consumer protection, environment, food and drugs, franchises, insurance, labor and industrial relations, motor vehicles, occupational and professional licensing, occupational safety and health, purchasing, securities, uniform commercial code, and water pollution. State offices also provide automobile registration listings, information on the operations of foreign companies, interstate trucking data, and lists of current litigation regarding violations of state law. Depending on what you are selling, any of these might prove useful to you.

A word of advice when dealing with city, county, or state clerk's offices: They are usually understaffed, and they have few regular dealings with the public, so don't expect great people skills from them. Be prepared to explain very clearly and patiently what you want. Don't expect fast service. Remember, particularly in their workplace, being nice gets you a lot further than being abrupt or demanding.

A fourth public source of information is the press. Newspapers and magazines are, in themselves, excellent sources of certain kinds of information, such as promotions, coming events, real estate, business trends, licenses, transfers, new business starts, want ads, stocks and bonds, and what your competition is doing. For instance, if you sell financial management services to professionals with flexible incomes and you read that the stock market is taking a dip while the real estate market soars, shift your new business efforts to real estate salespeople. They of course will be the ones more likely to come into sudden large profits in such a market and so will have a need for your services. The brokers are likely to suffer a slump in earnings and so won't be such good prospects for a while. I once sold a multimillion-dollar contract to a company by noticing that it was *not* advertising a particular service that its competitors were. On the basis of my observation, I was able to talk to the most senior executives in the company and to sell them the service they lacked. CEOs are frequently interviewed by various business publications. Whenever one of them talks about the positive merits of training, I phone them up to let them know the range of training that I sell. I've made several sales this way. Furthermore, many publications offer public archives as well, so that you can search through back issues for information that may help you to qualify a current prospect.

Finally, the federal government can be a very useful source of information. The Freedom of Information Act in the late 1960s made a great deal of information available to any member of the public merely for the asking. Again, however, you must be specific. Two agencies of the federal government of special use to salespeople taking a marketing approach to prospecting are (1) the Department of Commerce, Bureau of Census and (2) the U.S. Government Printing Office. (See the Appendix for addresses.) Data available from the Department of Commerce include all of the census data on the population as well as those on agriculture, housing, state and local governments, manufacturers, mining industries, transportation, and foreign trade. It has projections and reports available on manufacturing, wholesale and retail trade, service industries, construction, government finance, and employment.

The Government Printing Office, for its part, publishes *The Congressional Information Service Index*, which documents all of those companies that have been involved in congressional hearings. The *Index* is available in most public libraries, and a transcript of the hearings is available by writing the superintendent of documents. If the name of a company you are thinking of approaching shows up on the index, write for the transcript. You will find it a very revealing document.

Other federal sources that can provide considerable useful information are: the Securities and Exchange Commission (SEC), the Internal Revenue Service (IRS), and the Department of Agriculture (DOA). The SEC requires all companies listed on stock exchanges to file an annual statement (Form 10K) and a quarterly one (Form 10Q). Form 10K requires a financial statement, a list of principal products, the demographics of principal markets and methods of distribution, a description of competitive factors, and information on backlogs and fulfillment expectations, patents and licenses, the availability of raw materials, cost of research, number of employees, total sales figures, and income for the past three years. All of this must be provided for each line of business. Form 10Q is a quarterly report on sales, volume, prices, productivity, labor costs, and so forth.

All nonprofit operations are required to file a tax return with the IRS just as individuals are, but the nonprofit returns are available for public inspection. They include gross sales and receipts, total assets and liabilities, net worth, itemization of expenditures, and income. In contacting either the SEC or the IRS you will get much faster results from the local regional office than you will from the federal office. If you deal with farms, farmers, or farm markets, contact the Agricultural Marketing Service at the federal agency address. This agency is very helpful with farm concerns.

"This is all well and good," you say, "but I don't have the time to hang around libraries and newspaper archives. I'm a salesperson. I've got a living to make. I can't research and sell at the same time." I agree. Though, if there were no other alternative, I would promise you better selling results for every hour you spent on research. Fortunately, it's a moot point. There are two alternatives.

First, there are many on-line databases if you have a computer and a little time. Standard & Poor's ratings of businesses are available, as are Moody's. Value Line, a stock purchase advisory service, has on-line services. So does Dun & Bradstreet. CompuServ and Prodigy may be useful, as might Dow Jones. Mead Data Central even has an on-line update on legal affairs called *Lexis*, which is very useful if you sell to the legal industry or to those who are involved in current or recent lawsuits. The best source of information about what's available on-line would be the informal networks of personal computer user groups. They can tell you what's out there and how to access it.

But if you don't even have the time to crunch through on-line information, go to your nearest college. If it teaches business courses, go to the head of that department. If it doesn't, go to the head of the library. Ask if the college has a graduate or senior undergraduate student who would be willing to do a few hours of industrial research for you for a reasonable fee. There will nearly always be at least one for whom the money will be a great help. You will get your research done and at the same time generate a sense of goodwill for having helped a needy student. The college will appreciate you because it likes to interact with the local business community as much as possible. And you may build some very profitable and pleasant long-term relationships as well. I have used this system for many years and find it invaluable.

Commercial Sources

There are three good sources of commercial prospecting information: industrial research firms, list brokers, and businesses that rent out their customer lists to others. (See the Appendix for lists of sources of industrial research firms and list brokers.) By far the most useful one for salespeople is list brokers. List brokers operate very much the way travel agents operate—that is, they sell lists of customer names from a number of different sources for a onetime use by organizations that want to market to those groups of customers. They do not usually own the lists themselves but charge the owner of the list a percentage of the rental fee for brokering it for them. At any one time, it is estimated, there are around 250,000 lists available for use. The broker either finds one to suit your needs or tailors one to your specifications and charges you the fee the list owner is asking for the list. If the broker performs special services, such as tailoring the list or looking up phone numbers, an additional service charge may be levied.

If you decide to use list brokers, keep in mind that you are not purchasing permanent rights to the list but merely the right to use it one time only. Of course once you get responses to it, those responses constitute your own list which you may use at any time. But the original list is strictly for a once only use. Also be aware that most lists are updated only once a year and that an old list (more than six months old) may be too out of date to be useful. Ask for, and pay any reasonable premium for, a "98 percent clean" list. This is industry jargon for one that has just been purged and is freshly updated. Failing that, ask the broker when the list will be purged and wait until then to rent it. Finally, you will find list brokers under "Mailing Lists" in your local Yellow Pages. Try as many of them as you must till you find one that will build a list to your specifications. Be careful. Most will want to sell you a raw generic list. These tend to be too general for good prospecting use. The more tailored to your specifications your list is the better the results you will get.

You can, of course, deal directly with the organization that owns the list or lists. This is the second good source I've mentioned. Usually you would use such a direct source only when it specializes in a specific area that you need to prospect. For instance, R. L. Polk & Company specializes in gathering data on the automobile industry and it sells lists of automobile owners as indicated by state registration data. If that is your market, Polk would be more direct and simpler for you to use than a list broker. But, as with the airlines, it will cost you no less because the brokers, like travel agents, charge their fee to the list owner, not to the list buyer. Some list owners are so large that they have access to almost as many lists as a broker does. Dun & Bradstreet would be typical of such an organization.

Industrial research firms (our third source) prepare in-depth analyses of markets, competitive behavior in those markets, prospect demographics, mailing lists, and in fact almost any service you could legally ask for with regard to selling your services or products. However, this kind of personal investigative service is almost never available for a song. Like any organization providing personal service, the firms that do it charge consulting rates and so are probably beyond the reach of most individual salespeople. Still, you might profit from it as a group or on a companywide basis. And if it pays for itself with new business generated, you will feel it is money well spent. If you decide to use a researcher, be prepared to specify carefully who your ideal buyer is, how many of them you want, and when you want them. Also keep in mind that the data you are asking for should indicate, if possible, the prospect's buying cycle because your use of the information will depend on timing it to when each prospect is ready to buy.

Creative Sources

Like talent, creativity is a unique and special factor. How you will be creative depends entirely on you, on what it is you are selling, and on the market in which you sell it. But I'd like to share with you a few creative prospecting approaches that I've run across over the years. I know a young man who is single and sells upscale luxury cars, who never misses a chance to tell the folks he meets in singles bars what he does for a living. He says he gains between two and ten excellent prospects each month this way. He doesn't push. He merely reveals his work. If people are interested, they talk buying to him. If they aren't, he doesn't get a prospect, and he doesn't push it.

Quite a few salespeople I know take out personal ads in trade publications or local newspapers offering their services or products for sale. Such ads needn't be fancy. Want ads can be very effective. I've sold printing presses by inviting selected prospects to a banquet and entertaining them for an evening. If consumers are your market, sell to everyone who wants to sell you something. I've sold services to insurance sales reps, car sales reps, hardware store managers, gasoline station owners, real estate salespeople, and my lawyer and doctor. And, of course, I've bought from them in return.

I've often wondered why more salespeople don't take out display space at county fairs or enter their cars as an advertising float in the local Fourth of July parade. I used to work with a franchise salesman who always drove a racy sports car and wore flashy jewelry. He would go to malls and sports events to make videotape movies of his family and friends. Whenever anyone struck up a conversation with him about any of this, sooner or later it would always turn into a discussion on entrepreneurship and the opportunities and success potential in running one of our franchises. He paid for the cars, jewelry, and cam corders with the business he brought in in this way. The sky's the limit if you are creative.

The best prospector I ever met reads the stock prices every day. When he sees a company make a big jump upward, he sends the president of that company a bouquet of balloons. Then he calls to offer his personal congratulations. He tells me the door is always open because even presidents are curious about who would send them balloons. He has built a multimillion dollar business this way. Create a way to meet people you want to sell to and discover what and when they want to buy and you can build your career on your success.

3

Using Market Information to Prospect Effectively

Once you have garnered all of the names you'll need, either from personal sources, public ones, commercial ones, or by dint of your own creative efforts, you must put them to work for you. You have now completed the first three steps of marketing in sales that were covered in Chapter 1. You have specified who your ideal client is, set a clear objective for achieving the amount of new business you must have, and researched the marketplace in order to develop a base list of names to be contacted.

Putting Your List of Names to Work

Step Four, you will recall, is to qualify that list in order to narrow it down to those who appear to be the most likely to want to buy. We discussed several ways of doing this in Chapter 1. Choose one and apply it to your list so that it can be whittled down to a manageable size. I usually prioritize the list at this point, deciding on the most likely, less likely, and least likely (or convenient, or profitable, or whatever).

Now I can concentrate on the most likely to buy, most convenient, or most profitable chunk of names and still have the less likely ones as a backup if I need more new customers after I've contacted my most likely prospects.

There are two steps to contacting them: sending a mailing piece and then following up with a telephone call. It is possible to skip the mailing and to work directly with the telephone, but unless you are already a skilled telephone prospector it is much more difficult to rely on one step alone. Furthermore, statistics show that there is a synergy that develops between mail and the telephone that simply isn't there when you use either one of them alone. Telephone follow-up on a mailing will usually increase the sales effectiveness of the campaign by a factor of five.[1] That's a 500 percent better response rate than mail alone! Let's look at each step.

Mailings

One of the most common approaches to mass marketing today is direct mail. Yet it is still not often used by most salespeople. I'm not sure why, because used well, with good qualifying telephone follow-up, it is one of the easiest and most effective ways to generate a host of excellent sales leads. Several reasons for this reluctance have been suggested to me over the years, none of which really holds up to scrutiny. However, in case you are thinking of one or more of them, I'd like to take a few pages to discuss them.

The most common excuse I hear is that direct mail is expensive and the company won't necessarily reimburse for it. Mailings do cost money. A mail campaign includes the cost of mailing lists, materials to mail, printing, setup, mail stuffing, and postage. Depending on the size of the mailing, you might have to spend between $600 and $10,000. Most salespeople shake their heads when they realize this and say, "No way. Not me!"

[1]As pointed out by Murray Roman in his book, *Telephone Marketing: How to Build Your Business by Telephone* (New York: McGraw-Hill, 1976), p. 3.

Perhaps you are sitting there agreeing with them right now. If so, consider this. Selling on commission is the closest thing there is to being self-employed without actually being so. Being self-employed simply means that you are willing to run greater risks in order to gain greater profits. The self-employed entrepreneur gets to keep everything he or she earns, not just a percentage in commissions. Of course the costs of earning it must be paid, but entrepreneurs get to keep a great deal more than the rest of us. In order to have that privilege, they forgo the security of a regular paycheck, company benefits, and job security. Most consider the risk worth the trade. In fact, the majority of the members of the Direct Marketing Association are self-employed entrepreneurs. They are the folk who have made the risks of selling by mail pay off. If it didn't, they wouldn't do it.

Commissioned sales representatives, on the other hand, have the best of both worlds. They still have the company benefits and at least some job security (as long as they keep on selling), but because they run the risk of a fluctuating income that is dependent on how well they perform they are usually paid more than office workers. They run greater risks and so are better compensated. It is the essence of capitalism. No risk, no gain. If you are a "play-it-safer," then you are probably not going to be happy in a sales career. Certainly not on a commission basis.

Every day your company spends money on you hoping that, when you make a sale or two, it will get that money back and then some. It costs to give you a telephone, office space, company car, expense account, sample case, training, supervision, and clerical support. Your company gambles on you on a daily basis. You are holding down the one job there is that is closest to being self-employed, the one job that allows you to earn directly according to your ability. Are you unwilling to risk a small cost up front in order to increase your own effectiveness? Are you unwilling to put a little money down to back the same player your own company backs?

The problem isn't, "How much will direct mail cost?" but rather, "How do I minimize the costs so as to gain the greatest benefit from every dollar I spend?" We'll cover that in the rest of this chapter. But I have one caveat before we do. I do not believe in magic bullets. Even when exercising all the precautions and procedures I recommend, it is still possible to mount a prospecting campaign that fails to generate enough business to pay for itself. In my experience such failures have been rare, but the risk is there and that is why the highest rewards go only to those who are willing to take it.

The second most common excuse for not doing direct marketing (a mailing followed by a phone call to qualify) runs something like this: "I hate junk mail! I don't read it, I just throw it in the garbage. I don't like to be bothered by people on the telephone trying to sell me something, either. If I hate it, how will my customers feel? It can never work because people hate it so much." If similar thoughts have crossed your mind, then I have news for you: The people who send out the mailings and make the telephone calls know perfectly well that many of the folks they reach will react that way. Yet they continue to send the mail and make the calls. Why? Because it works!

Why Direct Marketing Works

There are three reasons why it works. First, direct marketers know that they cannot actually sell anything by mail or even over the phone. Those who are not ready to buy or who are not at least somewhat interested in buying will simply not pay any attention. These marketers are not even looking for such indisposed people. Their whole campaign has been mounted to select and reach only those prospects who are most likely to want to buy right away. The fact that they reach others has more to do with the limited ability of mass marketing to really zero in exclusively on unique individuals than it does with selling. These marketers are "creaming the list." They are looking only for hot current prospects who are, for the most part, already sold and are merely looking for a chance to buy. They don't mind the ones who say no so long as they reach the ones who will say yes. It's the premise of this book. People buy when they are ready, not when you'd like them to. Mass marketing proves it, every day.

The second reason that mass marketing works is that the clear majority of people don't mind being approached through the mail or by telephone. Despite many people telling me that they hate it, nearly all of the national and regional surveys that have been performed inside and outside of the industry indicate that from 70 percent to 95 percent of the people contacted by mail or telephone actually appreciate the contact, provided (1) that they are treated with courtesy and consideration, (2) that they might, indeed, be reasonably expected to be interested, even though they are not (that is, they are on the right prospect list), and (3) that they are at least partially familiar with the product or company involved.[2]

The third reason that it works (and the least important one) is that mass marketing is a numbers game. If you call enough people, some small percentage of them is bound to want to buy what you have to sell. This is the theory that drives the automatic dialing computers that many of us find so annoying. If you can call several hundred (or thousand) people simultaneously, sooner or later you will reach some who will buy even from a computer. Despite my respect for and defense of direct marketing, I am offended when I receive a computerized sales call because a computer cannot treat me with consideration and because, with such massive volumes of calls, the lists on which the calls are based can no longer be selective enough to be targeting me through any of my interests.

The fault lies not with the fact that letters were sent or calls were made but, rather, that the letters and calls were not sufficiently personal, considerate, or targeted to the customer's needs. All too frequently salespeople send a product line brochure and perhaps a form letter describing the benefits of whatever they are selling and assume that this is an effective mailing. It isn't. In order to capitalize on the synergy of telephone and mail, the mailing should include three elements (see Figure 3-1 for a sample letter).

[2]Murray Roman, *Telemarketing Campaigns That Work!* (New York: McGraw-Hill, 1983), pp. 248–261.

Figure 3-1.   Sample letter for a mailing campaign with a telephone follow-up.

Ms. Joan Martin
Lot & Cot Real Estate
Developmentville, Florida

Dear Ms. Martin:

   The *Tallahassee Times* recently applauded the rapid
growth in real estate sales in the Developmentville area
(Sunday, August 12, 1990, editorial page). County closing
records indicate that Lot & Cot is one of the most
successful, fastest-growing real estate firms in the region.
Such a sales climate and your company's growth record in
it are two of the best indicators that you might be able to
benefit from the unique sales training program that I offer.
The third indicator occurs if you are also hiring new sales
staff in response to your growing market.

   I would like to set up an appointment with you to
demonstrate how my program will shorten the learning
curve of your new people and get them out selling
productively sooner. When the market's hot you need
salespeople who are just as hot. No one wants the long
downtime involved in training new hires, and the average
time between hiring and closing the first sale is greater
than four weeks. I can show you how to add 10 percent to
your sales by getting your new people to that first close in
less than two weeks.

   I will call you on September 7 in the morning to
arrange a mutually convenient time for us to get together. I
would like to work with you and your people, and I look
forward to our meeting.

                                            Sincerely,

                                            Garry Mitchell,
                                            Ph.D.

Writing an Effective Letter

First, the letter must be targeted to a specific, carefully selected individual. The more generic and formlike the letter is, the less effective it will be. It must address the prospect as personally as possible. This is where the specifying and targeting of your list selection, as described in Chapter 2, begins to pay off. If you have been able to match three or four of your limiting specifications in selecting the prospect's name, your letter will speak to that prospect much more personally than a bland form letter and general product brochure will. Having only a full name, title, address, and a computer-inserted first name at the beginning of the letter is not enough. The letter must address the prospect's current state of affairs vis-à-vis the service or product you are selling.

Second, an effective letter should make a single, clearly stated offer. A general statement of product or service benefits is not enough. A specific offer should be made, such as an appointment, a rebate, special showing, limited offer, special service, or discount. The more general the offer, the less effective the letter. Furthermore, the offer is greatly improved if it too can be tied to the specific state of affairs the prospect is currently experiencing.

Third, the letter should name a specific time at which you will telephone to follow up on the offer you have made. If you have a large number of follow-up calls to make, it is better to state only the week in which you will call. If you can make all of your calls in that time frame, naming the day you will call is even better. And, if you are so well organized that you can succeed in doing so, it is ideal if you can specify the time of day at which you will call. Whichever time frame you name, stick to it. Once you have promised to call at a given time, you lose credibility if you fail to keep to that schedule. Even if the prospect doesn't remember receiving the letter, or does but can't recall when you said you would call, your follow-through on your promise sets a positive precedent that can only help you in building a selling relationship with the prospect.

Finally, it helps to create interest if you can find a commemorative stamp that relates to the prospect in some way or, failing that, to your own business. Mail with an unusual stamp is much more likely to be opened and remembered than mail that comes with a plain stamp. Using commemoratives makes a quiet, tasteful statement about you and the way you do business that can be beneficial.

Telephone Calls

Prospecting well by telephone is a skill most of the salespeople I meet need to perfect. However, working on the telephone is an interactive skill that takes role playing and practice to develop. I will discuss the essential elements and provide you with a few guidelines, but the practice will be up to you. If you follow the guidelines and practice getting them smoothed out till they become an integral part of your prospecting routine, they will enhance your telephone prospecting and make you more efficient at finding and reaching those who are ready to buy.

Preparation for Calling

Every call must have an objective. If you cannot write down on a piece of paper exactly what your purpose in calling the prospect is, don't make the call. As you will see in Chapter 4, a sales call objective is a statement that describes the response of the prospect to the sales representative's approach. In the case of a prospecting telephone call, your objective would need to be something like, "During this call the prospect will reveal his or her buying cycle to me," or, "As a result of this call, the prospect will make an appointment with me to discuss x, y, or z."

Such a statement describes the action of the prospect, *not* the action of the seller. You must frame such an objective before you pick up the telephone. Write it down and keep it in front of you. It is this action that you will close[3] on during the

---

[3]I use the word *close* advisedly. There are several excellent salespeople I know who avoid even the thought of the word because it implies some sort of ending to a relationship rather than the beginning of a new phase of one. I agree, but I know of no better word and so, with this proviso, I continue to use it.

call, so you must have it always ready and at hand in order to keep your call focused.

Most of us hate to have someone read a script to us over the telephone in an effort to sell us something. The technique is too impersonal and somehow seems mass-produced. We all want to be thought of as unique and therefore to be approached uniquely. So I don't recommend that you script out word for word everything you want to say in your prospecting call. But I firmly believe there are parts of your phone presentation that must be written down and placed before you so that you can read them when you need them.

There are, in fact, four elements in the prospecting call that give you "success power" if they are written out—and a strong possibility of blowing it if they are not.

Your objective is the first thing you must have written out in front of you when you call. As I've already pointed out, it keeps you on track and tells you what you must close on. This step alone will make you a stronger closer and a more efficient prospector.

If you hesitate, stumble, stutter, or say "uh" when asked what the purpose of your call is, you will lose credibility and undermine the objective of your call. Second, therefore, *you must have a simple, clearly worded statement* of what the call is about written down in front of you to smoothly read to the prospect to introduce your call. Such a statement must do three things. It must tell the truth clearly; it must do so in as

---

Preparing for the Call

1. A clear-cut, carefully defined objective for the call
2. A clear, simple statement of the reason why you have called
3. The planned sequence of qualifying questions you will ask
4. Planned and practiced answers to all possible objections

few words as possible (preferably in one or two sentences) because you don't want to waste the call in discussion or argument over what it's about; and it should end with a question to the prospect that maintains your control of the call and moves it into the screening phase.

For example, on the follow-up call to our real estate letter, the reason statement for the call might be something like, "Ms. Martin, in my recent letter to you I explained that your leading position in this active real estate market makes you a good prospect for my sales training program. I'm calling to set up a time for us to discuss the possibility. Are you currently hiring new salespeople to meet your growing demand?" I've been prospecting on the phone for years and I still cannot do this as smoothly off the top of my head as I can when I've taken the time to think the statement out carefully at my leisure and write it down to keep as a constant, dependable, instant reference. In fact, I just spent twelve minutes creating this statement and I made nine corrections on it. If I had had Ms. Martin on the phone without such a statement to rely on, I would have been lost. And I would have lost her interest and attention with my first "uh."

Third, *you must plan and write down for instant reference the questions you want to ask.* We'll be looking in detail at how to frame and make use of powerful questions in Chapter 7. Everything I say there applies with even greater force to the handling of the telephone prospecting call. Have you ever watched a congressional hearing on television? The men and women who represent us there take what they are doing very seriously. Their questions are all carefully planned, sequenced, rehearsed, and *written down.* Follow the model of your representatives in Congress. When the questions you have to ask are vital, don't trust them to memory. Plan them, write them down, and keep them before you when you screen for the prospect's readiness to buy.

About an hour ago, as I sat at my computer writing this, a telemarketer called me to sell me a service. She read a carefully worded script, extolling the benefits of what she had to offer. I was intrigued and listened and responded, weighing my reactions as she went along. Finally, she closed and I raised an objection, one I knew she probably wouldn't have a good answer for. Sure enough, there was a long pause while she apparently flipped through her call manual looking for something to say in response to my objection.

After a few seconds of confused silence, I said, "I think I got you with that objection, didn't I? You don't have an answer for it, I'll bet."

"Oh yes," she replied, rather flustered, "it must be here somewhere!"

I could hear the flipping of pages and then she began to laugh. So did I, and we ended the call on a warm, friendly, human note. But she didn't get her sale. She lost the call when she didn't have the answer to my objection at her fingertips!

So *the fourth scripted element must be your answers to potential objections.* When you sit down to the telephone to prospect, place in front of you the very best answers you can think of for every possible objection you can anticipate. There may still be one that you never even dreamed of, and when it is raised, answer it as best you can, but realize that the risk of losing your objective increases tenfold when you have to ad lib an answer to an objection. Only with carefully thought out answers ready at an instant's notice will you be able to handle objections smoothly, credibly, and most effectively on the telephone. Do it and your percentage of successful calls will increase dramatically.

During the Call

A frequent problem encountered in sales phone calls is the wandering prospect, the person who asks too many questions, or raises irrelevant issues, or sidetracks the call in some such manner. Once you allow the call to wander all over the place, it is very hard to close on your objective. To help keep you on track, and to help in planning your calls, let's look at the flow of a prospecting call. Figure 3-2 shows graphically the parts of the flow that are discussed in detail in this section.

Every call starts with someone picking up the phone and saying "Hello." So the first thing the sales prospector must

Figure 3-2.   The flow of the call.

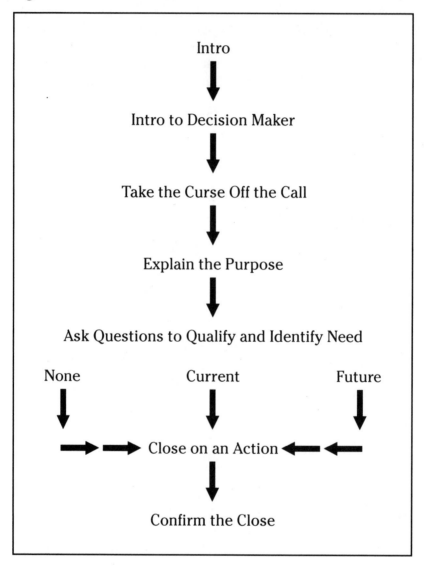

deal with is the introduction to the person who answers the phone. This is not a terribly complex issue unless you get someone whose business it is to screen calls and select those who will be allowed to talk to the decision maker you wish to reach. There are several titles such gatekeepers may have but most commonly the term "secretary" fills the bill because this is frequently one of the jobs required of a secretary.

People at my seminars often ask me, "How do you get past the secretary?" I wince whenever I hear the question, because the person who asks it is doomed to failure with that attitude.

"How would you respond to someone who approached you as if you were some sort of barrier or obstacle to 'get past'?" I ask.

"I'd be pretty defensive, I guess," they answer.

"Then why do you want to create a defensive posture in that secretary? Wouldn't it be more to your advantage if he or she were friendly and responsive?" I say.

"Yes," they admit, sometimes rather grudgingly.

But of course it's true. All of us are defensive when we are attacked or when we suspect someone is attempting to slip around and outflank our position. Secretaries are no different. They are charged with screening calls for their bosses. If you try to sneak around them, they will do everything in their power to stop you. Is that any way to sell? Of course not.

The very first step that a salesperson must take when a screening person answers the phone is to forget the decision maker and sell the screener. You must make yourself someone that secretary or assistant wants to put through to the boss. There are several things you can do to accomplish this:

• Ask for and use the secretary's name. No one wants to be thought of as an object. Call a secretary by name so that he or she will be able to respond to you in the same manner.

• Put a little intimacy into the call. I don't mean by that that you should be fresh or insinuating, but merely friendly. Be warm and smile while you talk. If there is a natural opening for it, kid the screener, as I did the telemarketer who couldn't answer my objection. Once the other person responds as a person and not as a gatekeeper, you have the beginnings of a relationship.

• Use your prepared explanation of the purpose of the call if it makes sense to do so. If not, because you have stated that you will call at this time in your mailing piece, you can comfortably and honestly say that so-and-so is expecting your call, or that it is in reference to your previous correspondence. Neither of these alternatives is as good as having a purpose statement ready to explain your call, but either will work fairly well.

• Use the phrase, "Maybe you can help me." If there is a magic bullet in sales, this is it. It is difficult for people to remain defensive when someone openly asks for our help. Doing so takes away defensiveness. Don't beg by saying, "Please, help me," though. Pleading undermines the authority you must project in order to maintain credibility. The first phrase, however, does not undermine you; rather, it is a polite, assertive request for help.

• Be as honest and open as you can be with the screening secretary. I usually say something like, "I'm interested in doing business with so-and-so (the boss). What would be the best way for me to go about that?" Now we have a dialogue that recognizes the secretary's role as gatekeeper and respects it. I can ask a number of questions once that dialogue is opened and establish a great deal of background information on my prospect that will let me know where he or she is in the buying cycle. I am constantly surprised by the fact that the secretary will often tell me much more than the boss will. But an open and honest relationship must be established first.

I have given and still give a number of seminars to secretaries. I ask them, "When salespeople call to talk to the boss, which ones are you most inclined to put through?" Invariably they answer, "The one who is honest and straight-forward, who doesn't play sneaky games or try to trick me." So befriend the screener if you can. You will be far more likely to succeed than you will be by trying to "get past" him or her.

Of course it is always possible that the decision maker is busy, absent, or not available to talk to you for some other reason. Always be prepared to arrange for a callback or to leave a well thought-out message. This step will take care of that other annoying inevitability, the answering machine. People tell me that they hate them. There is no need to if, before you call, you write down the message you will leave if the person you want isn't there. Then it's simple to leave them with a message that is designed to induce them either to call you back or to want to talk to you when you call again.

So, for the first event in the flow of the call, the introduction to the person who answers the phone, you need to (1) have a purpose statement written out in front of you, (2) ask for and use the answerer's name, (3) have a prepared strategy for gaining his or her cooperation, (4) have a prepared message to leave if you need to, and (5) be prepared to arrange a time for a callback.

The second event in the flow of the call is your introduction to the decision maker. The research I referred to earlier, cited by Murray Roman, indicates that people respond well to names with which they are familiar. So, if you represent a name-brand product or service, a well-known company or product line, a currently newsworthy or controversial line, use that familiar information up front. Say, "Mrs. Jones, this is so-and-so from (or representing) *(the well-known name)"* Don't mention dealer names or distributor names, because these only confuse. Just the well-known name and your own.

The problem is simply that few people listen carefully. Most people only listen for key sounds or stressed syllables in familiar words, assume the meanings they impart to those sounds, and ignore the unstressed syllables or less prominent sounds. This is why people often think they have heard what the speaker denies saying, or why they wonder, when what they have said seems clear enough to themselves, why their listeners behave as if they had said something else. Unfamiliar sounds require more concentration and careful listening. Yet few people devote that necessary extra concentration to the opening words of a stranger on the telephone. So, saying a name that is familiar is much more likely to get attention and focus the listener than if you were to give an unfamiliar name.

By the same token, it is therefore mandatory that you enunciate your own name clearly and carefully when introducing yourself. This is particularly true when the person you are calling is not of the same linguistic background that you are. If you have a common Anglo-Welsh name like Jones, you will be easily understood by those who are adept at speaking English. But a Spanish-speaking prospect, for whom the sound *J* doesn't exist, would have to make a mental adjustment to understand you. So would a native French speaker. And most people do not pick up the phone ready to do that. So, state your own name with care and use the most familiar brand name you can when you introduce yourself to the prospect.

Telephone calls invariably interrupt whatever someone is doing when the phone rings. This fact provides you with the opportunity to deliver a highly considerate relationship-building message to your prospect. Questions like, "Do you have a moment?" or, "Did I take you away from something urgent?" or, "Is this a convenient time?" remove the "curse" from the call. They express empathy for the prospect, a desire not to intrude, and a courteous willingness to accommodate to the prospect's sense of urgency or availability. At the same time, they make no apology for calling and in no way undermine your position as a seller of goods or services that the prospect will want to buy. So the third event in the flow of the call is to take the curse off it by gaining permission to proceed.

The fourth step is to explain the purpose of the call. Frequently when you ask, "Did I reach you at a convenient time?" the answer will be "What's it about?" Even if the question isn't asked directly, it will be in the prospect's mind and so must be answered as soon as possible. So, regardless of what the reply to your "curse remover" is, respond by explaining why you made the call. Here is where you will use your well-thought-out written statement of what the call is about.

Remember, you don't want to get sidetracked into a lengthy explanation or, worse, an argument at this point. It is best, therefore, to end your short one- or two-sentence statement of your purpose with a question. Doing so requires the prospect to respond to you, rather than ask questions, and so allows you to maintain control of the call and move to the next stage: screening and qualifying. Notice that in our real estate example I ended the explanation with the question, "Are you currently hiring new salespeople to meet your growing demand?" Ms. Martin must either answer my question, thus allowing me to continue the screening and qualifying step, or completely change the subject by asking me about what I'd said before asking the question. Because that is a much more difficult response, most people usually just answer the question.

You will recall that on a prospecting call you are merely trying to establish whether or not your initial demographics are correct and if this person is indeed a likely prospect for you. You need to ask screening questions that qualify prospects so you will know whether to close directly for an appointment, establish contact later when they will be in the market, or correct your prospect list by eliminating those names that are clearly not good prospects at all. In other words, you are attempting through your questions to discover the prospects' needs for what you sell and the time frame in which they buy.

There are three possible answers: They have a current need, a future need, or no need. Be prepared to respond to each one appropriately. If the need is current, they are ready to buy and are therefore excellent prospects. Close for an appointment as soon as is conveniently possible. If they have a future need but are simply not ready to buy yet, close for permission to recontact them at the time they indicate they will probably be ready. And in case they have miscalculated, get back to them a month or so before that time merely to establish contact prior to their intensive shopping around. If there is no need, I usually ask for a referral or close for permission to at least put them on my mailing list to be contacted on a low-priority basis in case their needs change in the future. In any case, your objective will frame what it is that you want to close on, and which of these three categories their responses fall into will best determine your close.

Once you have established what the need is, you can close to satisfy it. This is the action step, the sixth, in the flow of the call. It is where you ask the customer to do something and, as mentioned earlier, it must be an action on the part of the prospect, not the salesperson. Your carefully framed and written-out objective will key you into this step.

One of the most frustrating events in sales is being stood up by no-show prospects. I find it exceedingly annoying personally and often speculate on what it is that would allow a prospect to behave with such a lack of consideration for the salesperson. Consequently, the final step in the flow of the call is to confirm with the prospect the action on which you have closed. If the prospect repeats to you what the arrangements are, the chances are much greater that he or she will show up at the appointed time. It isn't enough to get prospects to say merely, "Okay," or, "Uh-huh." You gain a much stronger confirmation if you get them to respond to requests such as:

> "Let me give you directions [if they are coming to you]. Do you have a paper and pencil? Good, then here's what you do . . ."
> "Let me see if I have the directions right [if you are going to them]."
> "Let me give you my phone number in case, for any reason, your plans change and you have to reschedule our appointment. Do you have a paper and pencil handy? Good, then write this down . . ."

Never assume that your prospects have paper and pencil. Always ask if they are handy. That way they are much more likely to write down the information you give and, consequently, to keep the appointment. Notice that you are asking here for some form of involvement on their part in the commitment step. If you are comfortable in doing so, you might want to make an intentional mistake in feeding back to them the date, or time, or directions. If they intend to take the appointment seriously (and they will if they're ready to buy), they will correct you. If they fail to correct you, correct yourself and ask them to verify if your correction is right.

From time to time I find salespeople who say that they feel uncomfortable "playing tricks" on their prospects. If you are such a person with regard to these last two techniques, remember that your whole purpose in prospecting is to discover whether or not the prospect is ready to buy what you're selling. You do not want to make a presentation to someone who isn't ready or to pressure someone who really doesn't want to buy from you right now. Many people, accustomed to high-pressure sales pitches, or afraid that they may be subject to one, will agree to anything to get rid of a caller and then just not show up for the appointment. Far from being "tricks" you play on prospects, these techniques are subtle, courteous ways of establishing the level of commitment of those prospects and of confirming their desire and readiness to buy.

Once you have set up an appointment with your prospect, you must begin to plan what you are going to say and do when you meet. The following chapters will cover how to create a sound relationship in face-to-face sales interviews and how to handle the difficulties that sometimes arise, and will consider these subjects from the viewpoint of the customer's readiness rather than from that of the sales representative's desires.

4

The Heart of the Sale: Call Objectives

Have you ever wondered why it is that some folks seem to be able to close sales easily while others appear to struggle forever to bring in an order? We all know the superstars of our business, the salespeople who time after time succeed in coming in over quota, who always outproduce nearly everyone else. Yet a much larger group of salespeople takes the same training courses, works in the same industries, prospects in the same territories, but just never seems to be able to close as effectively. This difference in performance has fascinated me for a long time, so about five years ago I set out to discover the reasons for it. Obviously, the star performers were doing something that the others were not. I needed to find out what it was.

I talked to sales managers, their star performers, and regular salespeople. Probably the most frequently mentioned complaint of sales managers was, "My people just aren't aggressive enough at closing. They accept 'no' too easily. They just seem to quit too soon." The second-most-common problem they defined was that most of their salespeople "just didn't seem to know when to close. The customer is ready, asks a surefire closing question, and the sales rep just keeps right on talking through it and loses the sale." When managers look for new salespeople they always try to discover how strongly the candidate will close. Pick up any newspaper and turn to the help wanted ads under sales. Ad after ad will demand a "strong closer."

The strong closers I talked to, for their part, didn't seem to know exactly what it was they did that made them successful in getting the orders. Each one felt it was something different. Some even shrugged and said, "I dunno. I've always been lucky, I guess. I just sort of have this feeling when it's right, you know?" which, of course, didn't help me much. When I went to the regular performers, they told me that they did everything they were taught to do and had no idea why they weren't as successful as "those other guys are." But in talking to them, I detected a difference. The regulars talked about closing the sale. They were concerned with what they were saying and doing and whether or not they were following the techniques they'd learned in training. They wanted very much to "do it right," to make it happen. They looked for "buying signals" and practiced "handling objections."

The superstars, on the other hand, weren't concerned with these things. They had an entirely different mind-set. They didn't bother with the specifics of what they were doing during their sales calls. From start to finish, their total concentration, to the exclusion of everything else, was on the effect they were having on the prospect or customer. It was the *customer's* behavior that interested them, not their own! When they went in to sell, they went in to get the customer to respond in ways that would lead them naturally to the close. What they did to effect that would vary from call to call. Technique, as such, was immaterial. What counted was focus on the customer's responses to their sales efforts and a mind-set that remained flexible and sensitive to those responses.

The key to such a mind-set isn't how one closes or how one answers objections. It starts much earlier in the sales process. It starts with the sales call objective. A properly framed objective defines the action you want from the customer and allows you to concentrate on monitoring the customer's response to what you are saying, to what you are doing, and so enables you to help that customer to make a purchase decision.

Goals and Objectives

There is frequently some confusion about "goals" and "objectives" that arises out of how each of us has been trained to define them. The procedure I'm going to give you here may differ from one you have already learned in another context. Old habits are often hard to break and it is my objective that, if my prescription is unusual to you, you give up your old way of looking at objectives and adopt mine. If you are reading this book in order to improve your closing ratio, you will need to begin to frame call objectives to achieve results, and to help you to do that, I want you to break any old ways of looking at them that you have learned elsewhere.

From a sales management perspective, goals are measured in sales volume. If you work on a quota system and have to make a certain number of sales each month to meet that quota, then the quota becomes your overall aim. This is not, however, a call objective. Your reason for choosing sales as a career defines your purpose, which can also be called a personal objective, but it cannot help you to close sales. There are many such goals in life that are frequently defined as objectives but that do not qualify as sales call objectives.

I call all of the aims just described in the last paragraph "goals." I'd like to reserve the term *objective* for the specific aim a salesperson has in calling on a prospect or existing customer. Your sales call objective answers the question, "Why am I making this call?" and, in doing so, it defines your purpose and so helps you to make the call more productive.

Of course I'm assuming that every salesperson reading this book already performs some kind of planning and preparation before making a sales call. Old-timers have said for years that the secret to sales success is to "plan your work and then work your plan." It is as true today as it was the first time it was given to a new sales representative as advice on how to succeed in this business. If you are not carefully planning your sales calls, in order to put any of the ideas in this book into practice you will have to begin. Chances are almost certain that you will not succeed in improving your sales if you don't. By the same token, it is most likely that by taking this one step alone you will markedly improve your sales performance.

From time to time someone will say to me, "Come on, Garry, you don't really set up call objectives for yourself, do you? I've been selling for years and I don't bother with them anymore. Why should I? I know what I want to say and that's all I need to know." The thing is that the people who say such things to me are never the top producers, almost never the really successful people. They are mostly the ones who eke out a living by "getting along" in sales. To all of them my answer is a resounding "Yes! I do set clearly defined objectives for every call. I even write them down."

Writing down your objectives gains you four strong advantages:

1. It forces you to concentrate on the objective of the call. It is far too easy to be distracted by personal problems, office decor, or even the status of the client you're visiting. Once you know your purpose you can concentrate on that to the exclusion of all else.

2. It is vital for you to maintain control of the call as you will see later in chapters 6 and 7. Many customers or prospects will attempt to take control or at least to distract the sales presenter, either inadvertently or as a defensive response. A clear-cut objective makes it easy for you to guide the interview back on track.

3. It defines your close. Many new salespeople (and even quite a few experienced ones) don't know how to ask for what they want. Frequently it is because they haven't defined what they want ahead of time. They hope that when the time comes they will recognize it and respond accordingly. This seldom happens. With a clear objective in mind, you can always ask for it.

4. It makes you a stronger, more assertive closer. "No" is

sometimes a legitimate answer. But accepting "no" too soon or too easily is the single most common cause of lost sales. Persistence sells. And persistence is much easier when you have a clear objective to use as a measure of your progress.

Objectives and Methods

Sooner or later in each of my sales seminars I will say to a participant, "You're about to call on a new prospect whom you've never met before. You have talked with her on the telephone, but this is your first face-to-face meeting. What is your objective going to be on this call?"

"Well," the participant replies, "I'd want to sound her out. I'd try to create a little rapport with some small talk, and then I'd start to probe to find out what her needs are so I'd know what to sell her. And, depending on what she told me, I might want to close for another appointment in the future, or I might make a presentation right there if she seemed ready. It would depend, you know, on where she was at. I'd play it by ear, I guess."

Time after time I'll get an answer substantially like that. It is, after all, the normal response to my question. Most salespeople would respond the same way. Yet nothing this participant has said constitutes an effective sales call objective. Let me ask you: What is the purpose of calling on a prospect or a customer? Stop reading for a minute or two and think about it. Why make a sales call at all?

If you answered, "To sell something," you are wrong! Remember, if they are not thirsty they won't drink; if they are not hungry they won't eat; and if they are not in the market they won't buy. If you answered, "To find out if they are in the market," you're closer, but you still don't have a sales call objective. Your sole objective whenever you make contact with customers or prospects is to get a *planned response* from them. In other words, you contact prospects or customers *to get them to do something*. After all, are you paid for what you do, or for how the customer responds to what you do? I've never worked for a sales organization that would pay me to make sales calls without getting results. And the results they invariably wanted were orders. Not promises, or excuses, or descriptions of what I did, but *orders signed by the customer*. Period. A sales call objective is a description of what the prospect or customer will do, of what action he or she will perform, because of your call.

The objective of the problem situation presented to the seminar participant is: "During this call the prospect will respond warmly and build rapport with me; she will describe her needs with regard to what I am selling; she will indicate where she is in her buying cycle and, as a result of the call, she will agree to a specific time for me to return and present my solution to her problems."

"So, isn't that what the participant said?" you ask. No, it isn't. Read the typical answer again and then read the prospect-oriented one. Look at the difference. The first one describes in vague terms the methods the salesperson will employ during the call. It tells about what the seller will do. The second one describes what the prospect will do. And as I've pointed out, the only reason you call on prospects is in anticipation of their doing something, taking some action. You have presented yourself at their door and, merely because you are there, they will react. They will do something. The point is that they should be doing what you want them to do, not whatever spontaneously occurs to them. By describing the specific actions you want of them, you can better direct your own behavior toward achieving such a result. You are better able to remain in control of the interview.

This may appear to be a relatively easy switch to make: moving from thinking about what you want to do to what the prospect's or customer's response to what you do will be. Unfortunately, it is a lot easier to understand the principle than it is to practice it. The problem is that we habitually think from our own perspective. Each of us lives, and therefore acts, from inside our own self-centered world. Infants learn to cry for what they want. Older children cry for what they cannot have. Teenagers demand satisfaction of personal "needs" from their parents. Asking them to consider their poor parents' problems is met with amazement. "What does that matter?" they ask. "I need it."

The habit doesn't miraculously go away when we reach our majority either. We tend to blame others when things go wrong. We expect courteous service even when we ourselves are surly and demanding. I frequently have to laugh at myself when I drive in the city and become furious with the stupidity of pedestrians who walk out in front of my car. But, once I have parked the car, I almost instantly become outraged by the reckless driving of the idiotic motorists who nearly run me down. A simple shift in viewpoint changes my attitude completely. Yet, even knowing this to be so, I constantly have to remind myself to stop seeing the world exclusively from where I am standing and to imagine how it must look from the other person's perspective.

One of the prime benefits of framing sales call objectives as actions the prospect or customer will perform is that in this way we can remind ourselves before every call that what we want depends solely on what the customer perceives as his or her needs, and that our customer isn't thinking for one moment about our needs. Customer-centered objectives force us to remain aware of the customers' mind-set and to recognize that they can only buy when they are ready. Customer-centered objectives are, therefore, the heart of an effective sales call.

Creating Sales Call Objectives

Most people ask at this point, "So, what customer action do I describe? How do I know what action to define as my objective?" There are two ways to delineate what responses you want from the customer (or prospect if it is a first-time call). The first is simply to ask, "What do I want the customer to do?" Whatever your answer is becomes your objective. However, that answer must be specific. For example, "I want the customer to buy my product" may well be the truth but it is far too vague. "Buy my product" involves too many actions on the part of the customer for it to be a useful objective. When your answer to the question is too vague, you must ask yourself a series of qualifying questions to break your objective down into specific steps. "What does the customer have to do in order to buy my product?" "How will I know when the customer has done these things?" "Why should the customer be willing to do these things right now?" "How many of them can I reasonably expect the customer to do on this call?" "What action can I settle for if the customer doesn't want to give me what I want today?"

These questions can be formalized into a standard procedure for creating call objectives.

1. Decide on the Appropriate Action

The three major criteria for appropriate actions are that they must be specific, observable, and realistic. This means that you will need to state exactly what you want from the customer. The customer will:

- Return my smile
- Agree to spend a few minutes with me
- Build rapport with me[1]
- Respond openly to my questions
- Tell me about his or her business operations
- Share problems honestly
- Agree to allow me to explore the specific problem areas that come up
- Agree to accept and respond to a proposal from me
- Agree to a future meeting
- Set and confirm the date of a future meeting
- Provide me with the entree to others I need to see in the company
- Sign the order I will present

[1]Note that this objective describes the customer as building the rapport, not the salesperson. This phrasing and practice will seem strange at first and, of course, the salesperson is trying to build rapport with the customer, but that effort doesn't count unless the customer responds actively by accepting the salesperson's behavior and reflecting it. That is, he or she actively builds rapport with the salesperson.

All of these describe specific actions the salesperson can logically expect the customer to take, and so they are all possible call objectives. They also meet the other two criteria: They are clearly actions the salesperson can observe the customer either performing or failing to perform, and so can be used to evaluate to what extent the objective is or is not being achieved; and they are all realistic. Too often, inexperienced salespeople set high expectations for themselves only to be disappointed when they try to close and fail. You should be able to gauge how far a prospect is able to move at any given stage of the sale. (If you don't feel confident that you can at this point, you will get more help in chapters 6, 7, and 8.) To ask for an action that the prospect isn't yet ready to take is to invite refusal and to be stereotyped as selling too hard, being too pushy.

2. Create a Rationale to Justify That Action

No one wants to be a "pushy salesman." As a result, most newcomers to selling (and quite a few old-timers as well) feel some degree of discomfort in closing, in actually asking the prospect or customer to do something. Creating a rationale for doing so will provide the double service of convincing the seller that this is the right action to ask for and that this is also the right time to ask for it. Properly justified, there is no action that should cause the asking sales representative even a moment's hesitation. If it does, then either the sales rep has not taken the time to set a clear behavioral objective or the one that has been set is wrong because the customer isn't ready yet, and the seller hesitates because he or she knows it.

Every persuasive appeal needs to have both an irresistible logic and a sound rational justification in order to work. So, once you have decided exactly what it is that you want of the customer, you must frame your request in a way that seems logical, that makes good sense to both you and the prospect, and that will allow your prospect to feel comfortable making the decision and you to feel comfortable asking for it. Creating a satisfactory rationale answers the often unasked but frequently present question in the prospect's mind, "Why should I buy this?"

Imagine that you are a new life insurance salesperson. You are calling on a twenty-six-year-old former schoolmate. To help youself and the prospect to feel comfortable with your call, you might frame your objective as:

> During this call the prospect will discuss and ask questions about the benefits that our insurance can provide for him and will buy a policy because by doing so he will be able to build financial equity to achieve his personal goals, and will be comfortable knowing that, if anything should happen to him, he would not be a burden on his loved ones.

This objective creates a mind set that provides benefits to the prospect, engages the prospect in rational discussion, and justifies a purchase on ethical, financial, and emotional grounds. Regardless of doubts or subsequent events, with this objective you can feel confident that you are providing a legitimate benefit and service that this prospect really needs and will enjoy if he buys. You will also find it easier to convey such a message to the prospect when you have spelled it out in this way.

3. Set One or More Fallback Alternatives

Of course it is possible that even with carefully planned and properly framed call objectives you may fail to get the action you've set yourself. When this happens you can always push harder to achieve that objective. That however, makes you aggressive and pushy and will act as a negative influence on the prospect. Furthermore, pushing hard now is certainly not aligning your sales effort with the customer's buying urge.

Or you can just give up and accept the fact that you've failed to achieve the objective you set for yourself. But that's nonproductive and only makes you feel miserable.

I'd never advise salespeople to beat themselves up over failure, so that leaves only one real alternative: Set a fallback objective that you can settle for if you can't reach your first objective. A fallback objective is simply an alternative objective that is usually easier to achieve.

If my first-line objective is to gain a commitment from a prospect to allow me to create and present a proposal that will address his or her problems, and I find the prospect for some reason reluctant to proceed, then I will have to be satisfied with achieving my secondary or alternative objective. In such a case that secondary objective might be:

- The prospect will frankly discuss with me the source of reluctance.
- The prospect will refer me to the other person(s) who might be involved in the purchase decision.
- The prospect will indicate acceptance of the potential usefulness of my service or product and agree to a future meeting.
- The prospect will build rapport with me.
- The prospect will indicate when or under what circumstances he or she might be more interested in what I am offering and grant permission to be contacted at that time.

These are not normally my first-line objectives on a call, but I use them all regularly as fallback objectives so that when I leave the customer or prospect and I ask myself, "What did I accomplish with that call?" I have a satisfactory answer and will not have to attack myself for incompetence for having failed to gain my primary objective. Furthermore, and perhaps even more important, I will have kept the line of communication open for a later date.

4. Check the Validity of the Sales Call Objective

Once you have completed the first three steps outlined here, ask yourself, "Is the action I'm asking these customers to take in line with what I know at this point about where they are in their buying cycle?" In other words, are you going to be tapping their real need to buy, or will you be creating a barrier for yourself and alienating them by trying to push them into an unnatural buying mode?

Then ask, "Is what I'm asking realistic? Can this person or these persons actually do this today?" One of the oldest pains in selling is wasting time selling to the wrong person or at the wrong time. I'd add asking for too much to that category, too. People will never move 180°. If they are diametrically opposed to you, try for 10°, or perhaps 12°. Then, on your next visit, you might be able to move them another 15° or 20°. Each time you see them, try for a little more. Eventually you will only have to close them 90° or so, and that's at least possible.

The third question you must ask yourself in order to check the validity of your call objective is, "How will I know when I have succeeded in meeting this objective?" Every sales manager and sales trainer in the world is familiar with sales reps who get so involved in presenting that they completely miss the prospect's moment of buy-in and continue to talk themselves out of a sale, missing the opportunity to close altogether. If your objective clearly states that the prospect will perform an action, the moment he or she has performed it, you have met your objective. Stop there. If you are not yet sure, ask the prospect to perform the action. It's easy to close when you know specifically what it is that you are asking for. Simply ask for it. The response will tell you whether you have made your objective, whether you still need to work toward it, or whether it is time to concentrate on your secondary objective. And remember, you are selling to achieve the customer's response, not the sales representative's desire.

That brings up the final question you must ask yourself to be sure you have a clear and useful objective that will guide you to stronger closes: "Are my secondary or fallback objectives observable, realistic, reasonable, and worthwhile?"

Clear call objectives are the bedrock of effective selling. If you don't know exactly what action you want from your customers or prospects before you even talk to them, then you are selling on pure blind luck. Sometimes luck will work. Most times it won't. A description of the steps you will take, of what you will say or do, may be useful, but it is definitely *not* an effective call objective. With the format I've given you here, and a little practice, you will begin to zero in on the customer's buying mood more quickly and efficiently than you ever believed possible. In the next chapter we will begin to look at why this is so.

5

How Buyers See Sellers

We have looked at a marketing approach as applied to sales prospecting. We have examined how to approach a targeted market segment by using both the mail and the telephone. We have discussed specific techniques for making the initial contact with prospects by telephone and booking appointments with them. And we have examined the vital role that a preplanned objective plays in a sales call. It is time now to examine what happens next. You have targeted, contacted, and set up your appointment with the prospect. You have carefully framed a sales call objective. You are now ready to make your first face-to-face contact with this prospect. What will you do?

The Selling Cycle

First, let's take an overview of the whole process. The sales call can be divided into five steps or categories of activity. These are in a cycle that usually occurs in an orderly progression from first to last. One or two steps may be repeated several times before you move on to the next step, but even then they retain their cyclical order.

Traditional sales training and sales literature approach all five steps almost exclusively from the salesperson's point

---

The Selling Cycle

1. Establish rapport. Gain the right relationship.
2. Find or establish a need the prospect or customer has that you as seller can address.
3. Present your solution to that need.
4. Negotiate the terms of the solution, commonly called handling objections.
5. Close the sale or ask for the action specified in your call objective.

---

of view. Customers are usually discussed in the abstract as though they were heavy objects to be manipulated by the right combination of procedures. If the seller has the right recipe, the prospect must buy. The most blatant of these approaches actually ask sales trainees to memorize, word for word, phrases and responses that "get results." I had a sales manager once who used to say to me (and, indeed, I imagine to all of his charges), "Just say this exactly as I'm saying it. Get inside my head and it will be just as if I were there talking to the prospect for you. You can be as successful as I am!" So we dutifully learned the recipes, and failed to be as successful as he was. Any such approach is doomed to failure simply because customers are not inanimate objects that can be moved with standardized tools. They buy only when they want to, need to, and feel comfortable doing so.

Let's look at each of the five steps from their point of view.

Gaining the Right Relationship

Put yourself in the shoes of the customer. Imagine that you are walking down the street and as you pass a used car lot your eye falls upon the most incredible automobile you have ever seen. If you love cars, this is the most magnificent, the most breathtaking vehicle you can imagine. If you couldn't care less about cars, this one is so ugly, so hilarious, that you simply have to stop to look and laugh at it. In either case, you walk over to the car, walk slowly around it shaking your head, perhaps even lay a tentative hand upon it. You look up and see this guy sloping across the lot toward you, rubbing his hands together and grinning. What goes through your mind at that moment?

Be honest now! What is your reaction? Most people at my sales seminars respond to this scenario by saying they'd run the other way. At the very least they would think something like, "Oh boy! Here comes this glib, slick, smooth-talking son of a gun who's going to try to stick me with one of these lemons." Honestly, wouldn't you feel the same way? Unless, of course, you are in the market for a car; then you'd welcome him because you want to buy!

Incidentally, if you sell used cars and are reading this and feeling unfairly treated, I apologize for picking on you, but I have asked in my seminars for years what the worst sales stereotype is, and the answer by an overwhelming majority is, unfortunately, "a used car salesman."[1]

People become defensive when they think someone is trying to sell them something. Everyone likes to buy: No one wants to be sold. So, in this first step, the happy salesman is approaching the prospect full of goodwill, wanting to create a warm, receptive, friendly relationship, while, unknown to that salesman, the prospect, having spotted his approach, is busily building defensive barriers and looking for escape routes and dodges to get out of the situation. This is so even when the customer is a purchasing agent whose job it is to see salespeople. I've never met a purchasing agent who didn't say (or at least believe), "I can't be sold!" Although they may not try to escape, they most certainly build barriers.

Again, when customers are in the market and ready to buy, of course they aren't going to build these defenses and

---

[1]And it is a male stereotype. If it makes it any easier for car salespeople, the second-worst stereotype is insurance sales folk, followed closely by men's clothing salespeople.

barriers. It is only when they are being sold out of season, so to speak, that they feel the need to fend off the salesperson. The sales representative who ignores this facet of customer behavior will not only fail to make sales but will also give the entire profession a bad name, and indeed has already done so. One of the reasons for customers' shying away from being sold is that experience has taught them that they need to.

Therefore it is imperative that you create the right relationship as early as possible with the new prospect. Perhaps the best description of what I believe the right relationship to be was given to me by one of my own customers: "A salesman should be like an English butler," he said, "courteous, attentive, responsive, very knowledgeable, firm, authoritative, and totally devoted to the welfare of the customer." Not an easy task, but an achievable one all the same. We'll look at how to achieve it in Chapter 6.

Finding the Need

Back in the 1960s, IBM inaugurated a whole new approach to selling by training its salespeople to call on senior executives and decision makers rather than on the traditional buyers of that day—the purchasing agents, shop foremen, end users, and mid-level managers. For salespeople this meant making some major changes in behavior and learning a whole new set of communication skills. Xerox picked up on the model, copied it, and refined it into its now-famous "needs satisfaction selling" approach. It became the sales style of the 1970s and is still practiced by many sellers and sold as a sales training package today by a training marketing company called Learning International, which acquired the rights to it from Xerox.

Needs satisfaction selling, as its name implies, is based on the obvious logic that people buy to satisfy their needs, and so selling is really only a matter of discovering those needs and then satisfying them. I have no quarrel with this logic. However, in order to sell to satisfy a need, one must first discover what that need is. Needs satisfaction sellers are taught to "probe" prospects in order to find out what their needs are. This is where the problem lies for me. In my seminars at this point I ask my trainees for a show of hands on how many of them enjoy being probed. Ask yourself. Do you like to be probed? I have never found anyone who has answered yes!

Customers are no exception. They hate it. No one wants to be interrogated. I know that needs satisfaction sellers deny that they are interrogating prospects, but, unfortunately, so long as their motive is to probe, interrogation is what they are doing. It only ceases to be interrogation when it ceases to be a sales call goal and becomes, instead, a voluntary sharing on the part of the customer. Probing is not a customer action; it is a seller's action and as such tends to become unilateral and counterproductive.

Of course the salesperson must ask questions and must discover what the client's needs and wants are. But probing tends to build resistance rather than to foster openness. If the prospect is busy resisting the probe, one can hardly say that the right relationship has been created. Instead, the prospect concentrates on revealing as little as possible while the salesperson struggles to find out as much as possible. Whichever one wins triumphs over the other in a win/lose match that can hardly be called "selling."

You may well be asking at this point, "If I still have to ask questions but, at the same time, I can't probe, what is it that I'm supposed to do?" We'll talk in detail about how to handle the delicate art of questioning in Chapter 7, but I want to make clear at this point that the customer's attitude toward this crucial step in the sales cycle is completely different from the salesperson's, and so must be attended to.

The potential customer who wants to buy will appreciate the salesperson's well-phrased questions and the attentiveness shown the answers. The prospect who isn't ready to buy or who is unsure about whether it is the right time to buy won't appreciate this treatment. This tells the effective seller two things: (1) Do the homework necessary to ensure that you call only on likely buyers; and (2) if you are unsure of the prospect's need to buy, then finding it must become your prime objective for the call. You won't achieve it as fast or as effectively by probing as you will by getting that prospect to build rapport with you, to relax and feel open with you, to want to build a relationship with you.

Presenting a Solution

It is amazing how selectively we listen. For the most part, you will read every word I've written here. But if I were to stand in front of you and speak the very same words, you would probably pay attention to only about 20 percent or 30 percent of them! And those would be limited either to the ones you most wanted to hear or to those that, for some reason, triggered a memory connection enabling you to lock in on them. Couple this with the fact that the average adult attention span for listening is 20 to 30 minutes maximum and you can see why it is that we don't usually remember very well what was said in a given exchange, or why two people's memories of what was said will often be quite different.

Yet time after time I listen to salespeople make 45-minute monologues and call them presentations. Do any of us like to be talked at? No. And yet we talk at customers all the time. A sales presentation should be a dialogue, not a monologue. It should consist of questions and explanations and solutions woven together in a relaxed and simple fashion. If you force the customer to listen, he or she will remember only a small fraction of what you've said. If you engage that customer in dialogue, asking and answering questions, you increase astronomically the percentage of what will be listened to and retained. What you say can be argued with, or readily forgotten; what the customer says is written in stone. Make presentations a dialogue.

Recently I was talking with a client who works on a federal government project. He was explaining parts of the project to me and in doing so kept using numerous acronyms for the agencies or departments involved in it. As you may know, acronyms abound in the civil service, and government language is filled with them. I had to stop my client several times to ask what one or another of them referred to. What became interesting to me was that in one or two cases I had to ask more than once what the letters stood for. I would be told but would later have to ask again, and I practice what I teach. I am not a poor listener. The problem was that the client was speaking from his knowledge base without any consideration at all for mine. What was commonplace for him he thoughtlessly expressed in the common manner. Yet he left me confused.

I call this pattern of behavior "the math teacher syndrome" because in order to be a math teacher one must be good at math. However, when you are good at something it is usually very hard to understand how others cannot grasp things that are simple for you. Consequently, math teachers all too frequently teach too fast for those who have difficulty with the subject. In effect, they do what my client did. They tend to assume familiarity with the material on the part of the person they are addressing. In sales this math teacher syndrome is a fatal flaw.

Most of us are familiar with the old *features, advantages, benefits* model of presenting. For those who aren't, it is simply a concept of relating each feature of whatever one is selling both to the advantage that feature has over the competition's model or version, and to the benefit it provides the customer. For instance, anti-lock braking systems are a feature in some cars. That means they are something special to that model and so can be made much of in advertising and sales situations. Such a feature gives the model a sales and performance advantage over other cars that don't have it. Of course the benefit to the owner of a car with this feature is that the car stops faster and is safer and more maneuverable in dangerous situations.

The problem is that, of the three, only benefits speak to the customer's mind-set. Anti-lock braking is the best improvement in automotive engineering in many decades, but not because it is innovative or because it is special and only available on a limited number of cars at added expense. It is magnificent because it saves lives and helps to prevent accidents. That's why people buy cars that have it. With rare exceptions, customers only care about what your service or product will do for them and don't give two hoots in a rain barrel about what advantages you have over your competition or even about identifying the feature that provides the benefit. Benefit selling works. Features and advantages are like acronyms and math that goes too fast; they only confuse and alienate the victim who has to listen to them. Of course the exception to this presentation rule is the technically oriented customer who can understand and appreciate features or who wants to compare your product with that of the competition. But even these prospects are better sold on benefits than on technical razzle-dazzle because basically everyone wants to know "what's in it for me."

Negotiating Objections

Notice that I use the phrase "negotiating the objection," not the more common expression "handling the objection." When prospects raise objections, they are motivated by one of three things: They may have a true doubt about whether what you are selling is what they want to buy; they may be genuinely concerned that, although they would like to buy, some part of the package you are offering (the price, for example) is not acceptable in its present form; or they may be indulging in a polite form of running away. That is, prospects run away from sellers because they feel pressured and are simply not ready to buy what is being sold. So they automatically raise objections as a smoke screen rather than confront the salesperson with an unequivocal "no." All possible objections are motivated by one or another of these three alternatives.

Let's look at each one in turn from the customer's point of view. This means putting yourself in the customer's shoes.

Say your sales team has been through a commercial off-the-shelf sales training program but it doesn't seem to be having any results. Sales are still slumping and the individual salespeople don't seem to be any better at selling after the training than they were before it. All of the sales managers in your company report the same problem. You feel that a good advanced sales training seminar would be just the ticket, just what they need.

You come to me and say, "Can you give me such an advanced selling skills seminar?"

"Of course," I reply. "But I'll need to come into your company and talk with you and the sales managers and even with some of the salespeople in order to get a feel for the problem areas and for what specific aspects of advanced selling would be most beneficial."

You invite me in and I conduct two focus-group-style needs analysis sessions. As a result of these sessions, it becomes apparent to me that the problem isn't really that the salespeople need more advanced skills; they are quite knowledgeable and skilled enough to perform better right now. The problem is that the sales managers have never been trained in management techniques and are engaging in a lot of self-defeating behaviors that demotivate the sales force. This is not their fault. Each is a fine seller in his or her own right. But only one or two have the skills of leading, of managing other sellers, rather than of simply selling well. I conclude that your sales managers need further training, not your salespeople.

I present you with my findings and recommend that you hire me to devise and institute a sales management training seminar to address your problem. This is not at all what you were looking for. In fact, you are concerned that the sales managers in the company will resent you for meddling with their jobs and fight you politically if you try to do what I'm suggesting. And so you raise objections to my proposal. You have a true doubt as to whether what I want to sell you is, indeed, what you want to buy.

In such a situation your objection is legitimate. My task would be to persuade you that my solution to your problem would accomplish your objective sooner and better than the solution you originally had in mind. You want the problem solved. I am not persuading you to buy but rather to buy *my* solution. And so we negotiate.

The second source of objections is best illustrated by an experience I had a number of years ago while contracting with a builder for my first house. My wife and I had been shown a number of models by a perfectly charming saleswoman. We sat down with her to draw up the contract and choose the various options that would personalize the house for us and make it uniquely ours (a luxury one can only have when building a new house). The saleswoman checked off each of the standard options we wanted and noted the several nonstandard ones we were requesting, and then sat figuring for a moment.

"Here's what your new house will cost you," she said finally, showing us a figure.

"But that's much higher than your advertised price for the model we selected," I protested. We definitely wanted to buy, but we had a genuine concern over the higher-than-expected cost. It was a classic example of the second source of objections. I have never forgotten our saleswoman's answer to it.

"Oh, that's no problem," she said. "Which of the selected options can we remove to get the price back down to where you want it?"

"But I want all of the options," I whined.

"Well, they are what adds to the price. Perhaps there are one or two that you might be able to rethink?"

And so we began to negotiate. We finally bought the house, with nearly all of the beloved options, and of course we paid the builder's price for them. Whenever I mentioned price, the saleswoman helpfully suggested that I give up another of the costly options. Price was never discussed, only options, which my wife and I dearly wanted. This is not a new technique. In fact it is a variation on the one Benjamin Franklin first described in his *Poor Richard's Almanac* fifteen years before the American Revolution. Our saleswoman did it beautifully, and it illustrates the second objection format and its concomitant negotiation very clearly. Notice that, as the buyer, I am confounded by my own desires and forced to choose between what I want and what I want to pay for it. But all of the pressure is internal. I sell myself with the subtle guidance of the salesperson. So I admire that saleswoman and often use her sales skill as an example in my seminars, despite the fact that she closed me for list price, a rare accomplishment indeed!

The third objection is the one most frequently misunderstood and too often abused by salespeople. It is the objection stemming from fear or uncertainty. Take a moment and read again the sales interview in the introduction to this book. Mr. Wright is a classic example of the evasive objector. He even gets the subject off onto bass fishing rather than his telephone system. From the very first he says he's really not interested. Yet he mildly agrees to talk with the salesperson, which means there is at least a spark of interest, of doubt about his 1958 telephone system. But Dickerson fails to respond to that doubt. He operates on assumptions, ignores Wright's evasions, allows himself to get completely sidetracked, presents blindly, and finally puts unjustified pressure on poor Mr. Wright by coming around the desk. This in turn finally forces Wright into an open confrontation in which he expresses the negative feelings he'd been barely suppressing all along.

The objections raised stem from Wright's passive personality and nonconfrontational manner. He isn't really ready to buy right now; yet there is that seed of doubt. In effect, he would like a salesperson, or other advisor, to show him that he is indeed ready, that his business truly needs a new system. Dickerson was right. Wright is a prime prospect. But not for selling a telephone system to. First he needs to buy competent expertise that he can trust and relate to. He suspects that there may be a need but he has no one he can trust to advise him. This is his real need. He'll buy a telephone system from the first salesperson who succeeds in selling him on trust and a consulting relationship *before* trying to sell him a telephone system.

The thing to remember about this form of objection is that it is almost never anything more than a symptom. The objection itself is usually irrational or at least easily answered at a logical level. But it is almost never solved on that level because it is really about much deeper fears and not surface issues at all. The effective seller must read the symptoms, diagnose the problem, and respond to it rather than to its symptoms. We'll discuss how to do this and how to respond to each of the objection forms in Chapter 9.

Closing the Sale

Statistically, only 7.5 percent of the population at large is truly decisive.[2] This means that 92.5 percent, to a greater or lesser degree, need to be helped to make decisions. Yet no one likes to be rushed into a decision. We regard those who try to push us to decide as intrusive, and we resist them. But without help, many people will shilly-shally over a decision until it is too late and the opportunity has passed them by. This is the dilemma for salespeople. On the one hand, people need their help in coming to a decision; on the other, they resent any obvious effort the salesperson makes in that direction.

Think of the most recent major purchase you've made. What went on in your head—and your heart—while you were trying to reach a decision? Did you ask yourself, in your own inimical way, questions like: "Can I really afford so much?" "Could I get by with a less expensive model? "How badly do I need the xyz feature?" "Boy, won't so-and-so be impressed when he sees this?" "What will the neighbors think?" "Do I really want this one?" "How will my family react?" And so forth. You may not have asked each of these questions, but I'll lay odds that some of them went through your mind. Even if you are in the 7.5 percent decisive range, you probably considered at least the facts of the case before deciding.

Each of these questions reflects one of the three factors that influence the psychological pattern of decision making. We'll take a closer took at them in chapters 8 and 9, but for now, I'll merely introduce them to you. In order for any of us to decide to acquire (or do) anything at all, we must first recognize or feel a *desire* to have (or do) it. Even if it is something that we really don't want to pay for, like a visit to the dentist, a traffic ticket, taxes, or the repair of a fender bender, we must feel a desire to do so or we would not do it. Indeed, we all know of folks who put off paying the dentist

[2]*Human Communications Research,* Vol. 4, No. 1 (1977). As cited in Beverly Hyman, *How Successful Women Manage* (Boston: American Management Association Extension Institute, 1985), p. 124.

because visits to the dentist are unpleasant or who try to ignore traffic tickets, escape taxes, or drive around for years with a dinged-in fender because they don't *want* to spend their money on these things.

Desire is the most potent factor in any decision. It can be positive or preventative, but it must be there or there will be no decision (that is, the desire to make no decision is stronger than the desire to make one). Of course one can argue that no decision is a decision in itself, and I would agree. My point is merely that the desire to move in any direction or to stay put is a major psychological factor in coming to a decision even by default.

The second major influence on decisions is the logic, the *rationale,* that makes the decision seem "proper" to us. Facts, statistics, the logical structure of the situation—all define or substantiate the reasons why one direction should be taken over another. Thus, the rationale surrounding a decision becomes a most intense psychological factor involved in making that decision. Some believe that the rationale is the most powerful of the three elements. I feel, however, that desire is more powerful. After all, how many things do you buy that you don't want to buy but buy anyway because it makes sense logically to do so? By contrast, how many things do you buy because you want them, and then think of all the wonderful *rationalizations* as to why you need them? If you are like me, the second scenario is much more familiar.

Finally, every decision needs to be *justified.* We need to feel that what we are doing is the "right thing to do." This is why we often seek the opinions of others when trying to make up our minds. Many seek others' opinions even when those others know less about the decision than they do. Much advertising is based on this need for justification. After all, if Buff Chips, the movie star, says something's great, it really must be great—even though, with all due respect for Buff's acting ability, he may know next to nothing about the thing he is advertising.

Real authorities create strong justifications as well. When he was the United States surgeon general, Dr. C. Everett Koop sold a great number of Americans both on the desirability of using condoms and on the dangers of smoking cigarettes. Precedent, procedure, self-proclaimed authorities, formal documents, and channels all serve as means for justifying the choices we make, for making us feel "good" about our decisions.

Contrast these three buyer needs with the usual closing practices taught to sales personnel. If I, as a salesman, concentrate on what I want, on objectives that define the dollar value of what I'm selling, on working the prospect up to the point of closing, on handling any objections that he or she may raise, and, with dollar signs in my eyes, on throwing out trial and hard line closes as if I were casting for trout, I will fail in most of my efforts. When I do succeed it will be because, by pure chance, the customer has a real need and inadvertently buys from me despite my frantic efforts to close.

On the other hand, notice what happens when I concentrate on fulfilling what the prospect wants, on objectives that define a positive response from a qualified prospect, on helping the prospect to satisfy the demands of making the decision, on negotiating objections, on taking a reading on the exchange and collaborating in closing it to our mutual benefit. What happens, of course, is a selling skills revolution from the hard sell tactics of the 1970s to the consultative skills of the 1990s and beyond.

You may be saying at this point, "Oh, well, it looks real nice in print. It's easy to talk about 'selling skills for the 1990s,' but what are they? How do you *do* them?" This is the right time to ask. Let's start with the first of the five steps to selling we've just looked at in this chapter—establishing the right relationship.

6

Establishing the Right Relationship

All of us who have sold for a number of years have customers with whom we feel relaxed and at ease. We may kid around with them, talk about their families, problems at home, favorite hobbies, and so forth. We are, in effect, friends. It is a comfortable feeling both for the salesperson and for the customer. We trust each other and work well together with a sense of mutual respect we have gained over the weeks, months, or years that we have been doing business together. Such a relationship governs how each of us behaves with regard to the other and helps me, the seller, to understand my customer and better anticipate his or her buying needs and to satisfy them with exactly the right quality of service. This is the ideal relationship, the one we wish we had with everyone. However, in my experience these customer/close friend clients make up a very small portion of the salesperson's total prospect list. Furthermore, everyone doesn't buy everything we sell every day. Sooner or later, we must actively seek new business, establish new relationships.

When we do, we face the age-old problem of how best to approach total strangers in such a way that they will want to have the relationship with us that we want to have with them. Even with a solid referral, we can't count on the easygoing comfort of our established relationships. There is little or no groundwork on which to build. We can minimize the risk by doing our homework and approaching only the most likely to buy from us, but even then we must forge a new and productive relationship. And we must start quickly because customers, like the rest of us, make up their minds about whether or not they like us and can work with us in the very first few minutes of that first call.

The Predictability Principle

This is so, in part, because of what I call the predictability principle. As physical beings we are biologically structured to be on the defensive. When we perceive a danger, our bodies and minds automatically prepare to cope with it, either by running away or by staying to grapple with and defeat whatever it is that we see as dangerous. This is called the "fight or flight" reaction and it consists, biologically, of adrenaline pumped into the system as a response to a perceived threat. Adrenaline makes the heart speed up, it makes breathing shallow and rapid, it restricts circulation to concentrate in the lungs, brain, and large muscles, and it primes those muscles, making them tense and ready for action. If we don't use them, they act on their own and begin to tremble uncontrollably.

The psychological effect of all of this is that we feel afraid. Excited, but fearful. Yet in the case of a sales call we know there is obviously no physical danger. What is it then that both the salesperson and the prospect fear? It is uncertainty, unpredictability. We are afraid of things unknown and so we are cautious with unknown people. As long as we can predict what is likely to happen next, we can be comfortable and relaxed. When we know people and can predict their normal reactions and behaviors, we can be comfortable with them. But the further away from the predictable we get, the more of the fight or flight reaction we experience.

At one extreme, our reaction is noticeable and we admit to being "nervous." At the other end of the spectrum, in cases where unpredictability is only slight, we don't notice it—we merely adjust. So we are usually a little less relaxed in the street than at home, dining in a strange city rather than in familiar haunts, meeting strangers rather than joking with old friends. All of us feel these degrees of tension and take steps to counter them, to feel more at ease. Alcohol is a classic method for easing social tensions. Tobacco is also one but is now falling more and more into disuse, or being replaced in some cultures with other drugs. When we meet strangers we smile a great deal and laugh at commonplaces that normally aren't funny. We talk to reduce the tension of uncertainty, hence the habit of talking to ourselves under pressure. After all, one of the most predictable things in our lives is the sound of our own voices, speaking aloud our own thoughts. In fact the sound of almost any human voice appears to be soothing and relaxing to us. So we talk to make the world predictable.

When you call on a prospect, a stranger who doesn't know you, both of you feel—to some degree at least—threatened. Both of you will try to relieve that tension in some favorite manner, some way that will make the circumstances as predictable as possible. In North America we might offer to shake hands firmly, smile, introduce ourselves and look the prospect straight in the eye. We might make small talk about the weather or sports, or, as many fine salespeople do, we might find something of interest in the other's surroundings (something familiar to us, of course) and strike up a conversation about that. One of the most common ways of making others predictable is by making stereotypical judgments about them, putting them into categories with which we are familiar (male, female, artistic, black, Jewish, family-oriented, pushy, bossy, old, young, WASP, yuppie) and then behaving toward them as if they really were our stereotypes.

This stereotyping response to our predictability need can grow into an insidious habit. I recently made a sales call on an executive who turned out to be a lad who could only recently have graduated from college. I am quite large, have a ruddy complexion, a deep baritone voice, and nearly silver hair. I hold an undergraduate degree and two graduate ones and have taught college for many years. I am probably older than either of this young man's parents. Neither of us was able to relax during the entire interview. He would not smile or relax and remained rather wooden and distant throughout. His lack of responsiveness in turn made me feel uncharacteristically tense. I began to assume that my age, experience, and manner (factors that usually work for me to create a positive image) triggered a negative stereotype for him so that, instead of my relaxing him with a predictable credibility-oriented approach, I apparently intimidated him or at least put him off in some way.

Now that you have ready my description of this exchange, please read it again and notice this time how my own stereotyping entered into my attempts to find a comfort level of predictability (and in this case worked against me). Notice in particular the words I have used here to describe this executive. Now contrast them with the words I used to describe myself. To me, I appeared predictable and credible, warm and positive. He, on the other hand, appeared to me to be exceptionally young, a youth easily intimidated by a strong father figure. We were at odds because the image we each thought we were projecting was being misinterpreted by the other's stereotyping instinct. Once I realized this, I found ways in subsequent calls to begin to build a workable relationship, but the first meeting was shaky.

Until prospects feel they can relax with you, they will remain defensive because almost everyone carries around a negative stereotype of the salesman "who's going to try to stick me with something." This is not the first time they've been called on by a salesperson. No matter what you say or do, they will suspect that you are trying to manipulate them and they will remain on guard. Attempting to make a sales presentation to people who are busy analyzing how you are going to try to persuade them is almost always a waste of time. In order to make a successful presentation, you must first be able to convince prospects to accept you so that they can then concentrate on what it is that you are selling and how it will satisfy their buying needs. Because they must feel comfortable with the relationship in order to accept you, the goal of a first sales call is always to create a new working relationship. The art of selling to new customers is the ability to quickly negotiate a satisfactory, predictable, and mutually relaxing relationship.

Zero/Sum and the Win/Win Attitude

Selling is not a game, of course, but game theory can help us to focus our selling attention where it belongs: on the customer and his or her responses. In the 1940s and 1950s a brilliant mathematician named John von Neuman created a probability game using binary mathematics that became the operating principle for today's digital computers. In von Neuman's game, all activity is divided into two types, or categories: those in which one operation (or side, or player, if you will) advances at the expense of the other, which he called a zero/sum game (meaning one side gets 0 and the other gets a sum of one or more points); and those in which both operations (or sides, or players) advance together to the advantage of both, which he called a nonzero/sum game. In popular terminology, zero/sum is called win/lose and nonzero/sum is called win/win. However, one important distinction is lost in the newer terminology. The win/win game is also a lose/lose game. If one fails to make win/win work, both parties lose.

In order to become an effective player of the von Neuman game, to win consistently, one must master three skills: zero/sum playing (because many situations call for it), nonzero/sum playing (because, of course, many other situations call for this mode of play), and the skill of spotting which situations call for which mode. Let's translate the game into real-life situations and apply it to some common events. Most sports fall within those categories that call for one party to win and the other party to lose. Both football teams cannot win the same game. Even a tie is considered a loss by the players. This is also the case in tennis and baseball (where tying is impossible), bicycle racing, sailing, soccer, ice hockey, and nearly any other sport you can name. One cannot engage in any of these with the intention of helping the other side win without losing oneself. In a courtroom only one of the litigants can win. In fact the purpose of going to court (or arbitration) is to have a third party "decide" which litigant wins the suit. Only those with the "right" numbers can win a lottery. Only one contractor can win a bid. All of these are zero/sum, or win/lose games.

On the other hand, in a family dispute everyone loses in the long run if one party (even one of the parents) wins at the expense of the others. In a management/labor dispute, when one side wins everything, both parties suffer: the "losing" side by not getting what it wants, and the "winning" side by creating the bad feeling among the losers that prevents them from properly fulfilling their side of the contract, which they now find hateful. If a purchasing agent forces an unacceptable contract on a salesperson, that purchasing agent will most likely experience difficulties with delivery or service or repeat orders or even with the quality of goods or services provided. These are all nonzero/sum, win/win games. To play them in a manner that "beats" the other side is to create a situation in which both sides must lose. The only way to win a win/win game is to help the other side gain at least enough of the benefits its members want to allow them to be satisfied with the deal.

I had a client recently who discovered, by reading an article in a national magazine, that one of his suppliers had been charging him 15 percent above the going rate for goods while assuring him that he was paying the lowest possible price. You can imagine how he felt when he discovered that he'd been overcharged for years. He was beside himself with rage, not at the mere 15 percent or even the dollar value it represented but at the sense of betrayal he felt. My client withdrew his multimillion-dollar account from the salesman's company, sued that company for a refund, plus damages, and took steps to try to discredit the salesman throughout the industry. The salesman had put one over on the customer. He had "won" at the customer's expense, and in doing so had created a situation where both would lose. All selling is a win/win game.

There have been a great number of selfish sellers in the world who have sold win/lose at the customer's expense. The sales stereotype is very real and it has become entrenched only through the manipulative practices taught to, and practiced by, earlier salespeople. Let's look at what you can do to help to overcome the bad taste left in so many people's mouths by poor selling techniques, at what you can do to break out of the negative stereotype and to create a mutually profitable relationship with new prospects.

There are three critical issues in the first-time call situation and all of them relate to the predictability principle:

1. The new prospect doesn't know you, feels a bit uncomfortable with you, and so falls back on a particular stereotype of salespeople in order to make you predictable. Usually, of course, it is a negative stereotype. At the same time, you may be stereotyping your prospect in the same manner, leading to confusions, misunderstandings, increased tensions, snap decisions, and (usually) no sale.

2. The new prospect may not know you but is probably familiar with what you are selling through past experience, hearsay, advertising, or your competition and has an opinion about it. This may be an erroneous opinion.

3. This state of affairs will continue until you can gain the prospect's trust by moving out of the stereotype and providing that prospect with a reason to trust you.

To respond to the first issue, break the stereotypical mold. Don't act like every other sales representative who calls. Develop a warm, friendly style (not a slick one) with secretaries and other company workers (or other family members and neighbors if you call directly on consumers in the home environment). Be as honest and open and frank as you possibly can be. After greetings and perhaps small talk, I usually begin a call on a new prospect by saying "I'd very much like to do business with you. How can I best go about that?" The answer begins to reveal the prospect's need. Most salespeople talk to make themselves more comfortable. Don't. Ask questions. Get the prospect to talk to you. Everyone needs recognition and you can give it only by listening and responding to what prospects tell you about themselves or their operation. This is what I mean when I say that your objective should be, at least in part, to get the prospect to establish rapport with you.[1]

Start from what the prospect already knows and is familiar with. Establish credibility by leading the conversation to this area and showing by your questions and responses that you are informed and knowledgeable about it. Get prospects to talk about themselves, their families, or their business operations. Position yourself as a consultant, not as a hard sell salesperson. Take notes. Many successful sellers bring only a small notebook to the first call and leave their briefcases at home. In these ways you can break through the negative sales stereotype and help the prospect to look at you realistically, to see you as you are. This often takes time, but I know of no shortcut nor of any better use for my early selling time than by establishing rapport, demonstrating credibility, and breaking the stereotype.

The second issue is how your prospect feels about whatever you are selling. Despite your earlier research into this prospect's needs and buying cycle, it is safest not to assume anything. This is even more the case with respect to prospects' familiarity with your service or product. Ask questions. Are they familiar with it? What experience have they had with it? Get them to tell you how they have used your product or service rather than jumping in to tell them how to use it. If they have used it wrongly or have had a poor experience with it, you can pinpoint the problem and help them to solve it. If they are not familiar with what you sell, *don't* make a sales presentation. Describe briefly the area in which your product or service functions and ask how the customer is presently handling this area. Don't tell—ask! The prospect can argue with or simply disbelieve anything you say, but what he or she has said is "written in stone." And remember, the cus-

[1]If you are thinking, "But *how* should I do that? How can I ask the right questions to get that prospect to talk to me?" relax. We'll cover question planning, framing, and asking in detail in Chapter 7.

tomer will feel more in control and more at ease talking than listening. Furthermore, any misconceptions that may be harbored will be aired up front where you can deal with them credibly, not hidden away where they can easily trip you up later.

The final critical issue is trust. Do you trust strangers? Perhaps, but do you fully trust salespeople you don't know? Put yourself in your prospect's shoes. I even prefer my own barber to an unknown one. Still, because I travel frequently, I will use out-of-town barbers, but I'm always much more careful and ill at ease when I don't know them. Check your own feelings the next time you have a chance by talking to an unknown salesperson about a big-ticket item, say a car or a house. Observe the level of mistrust or trust you feel. Check yourself in this way with several salespeople and then sit down and list the kinds of behaviors you trust and those you don't trust in a seller. Another alternative is to ask your own family and friends or even your best customers to describe the salespeople they like and those they detest. Then make up your list and practice the good features of their behavior while eliminating the negative ones.

In general, the sales representative who gives a canned pitch is always suspect. So is the manipulative character who asks trick questions or tries to close too soon. The person we tend to trust is the person who respects us and what we have to say. I am much more likely to trust you when you've listened carefully and helpfully to my problems than when you've tried to tell me what my problems are. And the more I've told you, the more I'll trust you.

Here is a checklist to help you minimize the first two crucial impressions—the stereotype and the pre-set impression—and maximize the third—trust.

- Keep in mind that communication is a transaction. It takes two to talk, and each of you has an effect on the other.
- Work toward your clear-cut objectives, but be conscious of the fact that they are *your* objectives and not necessarily those of the prospect. Part of your purpose is to

discover the prospect's objectives and then to help to realize them.

- Before talking to prospects try to discover which topics interest and excite them and which ones are most likely to prove duds.
- Always try to communicate something the prospect will regard as valuable.
- Look for sources of resistance as the prospect talks.
- Remind yourself that *you* are the main message. If your customers don't buy you, they won't buy what you are selling.
- Avoid being a know-it-all. People respond more positively to someone who seeks answers than they do to some one who dictates solutions.
- Help the prospect to talk to you. Encourage disclosure by self-disclosing. Trust comes about as a matter of trade. You tell me your secrets, then I'll tell you mine. You can't give away the ballpark, but you can be honest, open, and sincere to encourage responses of the same kind.
- Be aware of your nonverbal behavior and of the messages your body language is sending.
- Anticipate ways in which the customer may receive what you have to say and be prepared for those reactions.
- Remember that feelings and emotions are usually far more persuasive than intellect.
- Think of your function as that of a translator. You translate the customer's needs into problems your services or products can solve. Then you translate those solutions into images and language your customer can understand and respond to.

Content vs. Relationship in Selling

Behavioral scientists tell us that establishing the boundaries and ground rules of a relationship is far more important in dealing with people than what we actually say to them.[2] In effect this means that *what* we say in a sales interview is usually far less important than *how* we say it. That's an old saw, but let's look at why it is also true.

A number of years ago social scientist Erving Goffman developed what came to be a very popular way of looking at human behavior.[3] He compared it to a stage play. Each of us has "roles" to "play," which we learn through our experience and through observing others playing similar roles. In addition, each of us has a performance "on stage" mode (or "region") and a "back stage" mode in which we perform our private behavior. We have an internal "director" who watches our performance and coaches us as we perform. The metaphor goes on to describe other facets of our behavior, but these are all that we need to deal with here.

The idea that each of us is playing a role is a very powerful tool for understanding selling relationships, and, in particular, it helps explain our habit of stereotyping each other. If, in my mind, I am "coming on" as a consultant who is helping the customer, being considerate, and in fact providing exceptional service, but my customer perceives me as someone who is out to stick him with a lemon, trust is unlikely to happen, understanding will be confused at best, and true communication will be impossible. Each of us is casting the other in a role different from the one actually being played. As a result, we are not even in the same play! Goffman's terminology is good because it allows us to see clearly how the relationship between the seller and the buyer influences the interview and is shaped largely by what each of us thinks we are doing and by what each sees the other as doing.

Obviously, it is not enough merely to decide that you are now going to be consultative in your approach to the customer.

[2]In particular, Gregory Bateson (with Jurgen Reusch) in *Communications: The Social Matrix of Society* (New York: Norton, 1968) and Paul Watzlawick (with Janet Beavan and Don Jackson) in *Pragmatics of Human Communication* (New York: Norton, 1967).
[3]Erving Goffman, *Presentation of Self in Everyday Life* (New York: Doubleday, 1959).

You must get the customer to recognize that you are playing that role and to respond to your performance by accepting it and answering with the appropriate positive role of the consultee. If you fail to get your customer to enter your play, you will have to enter his play in which you are cast as just another pushy salesman to be put off and objected to.

Fortunately, most of us play several roles at the same time so that if we fail in one of them, we may be able to succeed in another. There are always at least three plays on stage in any buying/selling situation. There is the formal business relationship of selling. There is also the informal, personal relationship of two people relating simply as people. And there is the hidden constituency that each of us represents and is responsible to, and that we are constantly playing for. Let's look at an example of these three plays in action.

The first play is the business one. In our familiar example, Lloyd Dickerson is an experienced sales representative for Technical Telephones. He is calling on Bill Wright, who is a partner in Wright, Wright, and Jayston, a well-established firm of public accountants. You will recall that Wright uses a very old telephone system that has none of the modern features and benefits of the Technical Telephones line. Dickerson wants to sell him a new telephone system. However, because of his old system, Bill Wright sees eight to ten telephone salespeople each month. All of them want to sell him a new system. He has yet to see any real need to buy one. This is the business situation. The seller's role is to appear professional, knowledgeable, and interested in the customer's welfare. The customer's role is to play the hardheaded, practical business type who's seen it all and "comes from Missouri."

The second play is the interpersonal relationship between the two men involved in the interview. Lloyd Dickerson is a confident, successful young salesman. He likes to move fast, makes quick decisions, sizes people up in a hurry and is often right in his judgments of them. He is very knowledgeable about his product line and is a determined and persistent seller. He tries to keep sales calls on a business level and doesn't like to get off the topic into the long-winded war stories of his prospects. He spends most of his time selling and hates to take time to "hold the customer's hand." He feels that's the job of his technical support and service people. He thinks Wright is an old-fashioned fogy who probably ought to retire along with his antiquated telephone system. His role, as he sees it, is to be upbeat, modern, "on a roll," charming, smooth, and businesslike.

Bill Wright, on the other hand, is a methodical and careful man. He believes in tradition and has always admired his father's business sense and ability to build the firm into what it is today. He is not a stubborn man and is open to reason. But he is a traditionalist and he likes to get to know people, even his own customers, before he feels comfortable doing business with them. He feels the younger generation is moving too fast and wants everything in a hurry, the easy way, without having to work very hard for it. He likes the clean-cut look of Dickerson and his businesslike manner, but he is tired of seeing young hot shot salespeople and having them try "juvenile little tricks" on him. He knows that sooner or later he ought to buy a new telephone system and that's why he agrees to see the horde of youngsters who bug him so. When he's ready, he'll decide on one system and buy it despite the pressure of the salespeople he has seen. He will not be rushed. He sees his role as that of the paternal curmudgeon, irascible, but with a warm twinkle in his eye. He won't resist a "good" sales approach, but he won't help much either. He is a friendly guy at heart who would rather smile and be warm than tough.

The third play is the constituency each actor is performing for. Lloyd Dickerson has a sales manager who probably learned his craft under Ebenezer Scrooge. This guy, Paul Trezinski, rides him every day. When he sells well, Trezinski either raises his monthly quota or cuts his territory. When he doesn't sell well, Trezinski bugs him constantly and comes out on calls with him, even though Lloyd knows he can outsell Trezinski any day. And Trezinski knows it too. Lloyd is the best sales rep in the branch and has won three sales contests and twice been named national salesman of the month. All the guys look up to him and come to him for tips on closing and so forth. He has to keep up his great reputation. To top it all off, the dentist says his twelve-year-old daughter is going to need thousands of dollars' worth of orthodontal work that his insurance won't cover, and his wife's car is really on its last legs and needs to be replaced. He feels a lot of pressure from his boss, his peers, and his family to make this, and a number of other sales, this month. He must play the role of the big shot for them, of the hot, successful, "I'll get this sale for you, just watch my smoke!" kind of guy.

Bill Wright, though he's sixty-one years old, has always felt pressure to live up to his father's standards. The old guy has long since retired, but he still sits on the board of directors of the firm, and Bill still wants to prove to him that he is a fine manager and can run the business well. Usually he succeeds. His dad only complains when Bill changes something that he had set up in years gone by. Of course, if Bill can prove that it's a sound decision, his dad will go along. He's no fool. But he is proud of the company he built and hates to see changes made unless they're absolutely necessary. The worst of it, from Bill's point of view, is that his father is sure to complain about the change at a full board meeting and embarrass Bill considerably unless Bill can really justify his decisions. Of course, as the operating executive of the firm, Bill must also maintain his authoritative and strong leadership image with the employees. After all, he is the boss. Finally, a big expense like a telephone system would probably mean that he'd have to edge up the firm's fees to pay for it, and business is soft right now. The new clients probably wouldn't notice the difference too much and might even expect the higher rates, but most of his old clients would be pretty unhappy about it. Still, it could be got around in time if need be. He feels that he is forced to play the role of a critical, impossible-to-influence, "I can't be sold a thing," extremely tough Boss (with a capital "B").

In effect, each of the two people involved has three roles to play. One role is the up-front businesslike person who makes rational decisions. The second is the hidden individual who "directs," makes emotional decisions, and expresses the "personality role." The third is responsible to others and has to justify his behavior to those relevant constituents. The effective selling relationship is built on all three.

In my own sales calls I strive to establish a bond of mutual liking and respect as soon as possible, and most of my communication early on is devoted to building, monitoring, and responding to the state of the growing personal relationship. At the same time, because I am selling professional consulting services, the role I must project is that of competence, experience, knowledge, confidence, and expertise. These are the formal business attributes that my clients need to see in evidence before they can hire me. I am thus operating on two levels, building relationships in both playing areas at the same time.

The third area, that of constituents, comes into play a little later. It is important to plant a few seeds in this area in the early stages by establishing who the constituents are and how important they may be. By asking about them you can gauge how the customer responds to them and how important this area will be later in the sale. But moving into it openly too soon makes one appear very manipulative and devious. For instance, one of my own cardinal rules has always been that I must make the people who buy from me look good for doing so to their constituents. But if I come right out and say in the first five minutes of our conversation, "Don't worry! Trust me! You'll come out of this smelling like a rose!" I would completely undermine anything else I have to say. Yet that is exactly the message I must get across to my prospects in order to help them to reach a buying decision.

As I pointed out in Chapter 5, only 7.5 percent of the population in general is truly innovative, willing to take a risk regardless of what others will think. The rest, 92.5 percent, to a greater or lesser degree, will hedge by saying, "Can I talk to somebody who has already bought one from you?" or, "Well, let me talk it over with my (pick one: spouse, lawyer, accountant, relative, friend, boss) and then we'll see," or, "Can I bring it back for credit if it doesn't work?" All who sell are familiar with such evasions. They are all expressions of doubt, pleas for assurance that by deciding to buy from you the customer won't look foolish to his or her constituents. It is called "buyer's remorse" and it stems from the fear of a negative response from the constituents with regard to the new purchase. It must be addressed, but should be tackled only indirectly in the early interviews with a potential client.

Specifically, to work with this third area of the powerful constituency your customer represents, you must make a habit of illustrating issues right from the first with effective examples of how others have used or are using your services or products. Provide documentation or samples of what you are selling. Old-fashioned as sample giving is, it is how pharmaceutical products are sold to doctors, food products are sold in stores, and all kinds of goods are sold at trade and other fairs. Provide references, even before you are asked to. Cite pilot programs or other industry users, especially the prospect's competitors. It is this buyer need that is being addressed when movie stars endorse products on television. After all, if Cher works out at a gym, it must be a pretty good gym, right?

Be on time. Take special care to show respect for the potential client's time, space, concerns, and artifacts. How you handle each of them indicates your degree of concern for the prospect outside of the arena in which you are selling but still inside the constituency circle. I like to ask prospects what their buying procedure is, how they came to purchase something other than what I'm selling. Their answers tell me who else is involved in the decision and who their constituents are and how important a role each will probably play in the sale. Finally, no matter how strange these constituents may be, they must be treated with the greatest respect. The buyer *must* be able to gain their approval for the purchase, formally or informally, in order to be happy with it.

For example, if Lloyd Dickerson had taken the time to add strong personal relationship behavior to his crisp businesslike approach, if he had asked more about how Mr. Wright's telephone system had survived so long, he would have found out who the constituency was, built a friendlier relationship with Mr. Wright, and, because he has a good businesslike approach, he might have made a sale. Certainly, he would have begun a relationship that could have led to one.

Controlling Nonverbal Behavior

The value of understanding nonverbal behavior becomes apparent when we realize that, for most of us, it is transparent behavior. We are unaware of it. It is as though it were invisible because we "give off" messages unconsciously and, at the same time, we respond to the messages given off by others without really being aware that we are doing so. This is why it is worthwhile for salespeople to understand and consciously project positive nonverbal patterns. Customers, as we have seen, are unconsciously looking for role clues and responding without thought to the ones they see. In order to create a positive, constructive relationship, it helps greatly for the salesperson to control the nonverbal messages he or she provides in order to influence the behavior of the prospect.

There have been many books written about nonverbal behavior. Most deal mainly with *kinesics*, which is the technical term for "body language." Quite a few deal also with *proxemics*, which is the study of how we communicate through our use of space. A few even deal with how we communicate by using our clothes and the artifacts around us, such as our homes, cars, furniture, briefcases, books, magazines, and so on. The problem I have with all of these books is that the best they can say is that we mostly indicate certain things when we behave in certain ways, but that this is not always so. Frequently we will do any number of these supposedly meaningful things without meaning anything. In other words, our nonverbal signals are ambiguous. It is impossible to say at any given time if a gesture means one thing or another. At best, then, scholars tell us, we must read nonverbal behavior in "meaning clusters" in which each gesture reinforces the meaning behind other gestures but no single gesture alone can be said to "mean" anything.

Using this approach unfortunately keeps you too busy looking at the trees to see the forest. After all, Shakespeare was not a great writer because he used good grammar or strung words together in interesting clusters. He was a great writer because of the overall impression his words made, because of his intent when using them. His meaning lies in the response of the audience or reader to both what he had to say and to how he said it, and not merely in the medium (that is, poetic language) used to communicate it. This is why each of his plays is still subject to ever new and different interpretations.

In much the same way, the meaning of nonverbal behavior isn't the specific gesture or gesture cluster; rather it lies in the response of the person who perceives it. All of our nonverbal behavior communicates our relationship to others and to our environment. We use words for most of our specific content. So our nonverbal behavior is a set of physical responses to how we perceive ourselves and our relationship at any instant to those around us. There are, for the most part, only three such relationship messages we communicate nonverbally: *responsiveness*, which means how much attention we are paying to others; *authority*, which means how we see ourselves and others in the pecking order; and *affect*, which is a psychological term for visible emotion.

Responsiveness

We are extremely sensitive to how much attention is being paid to us. It is not a natural sensitivity but a learned one. Children are usually quite unconscious of others until they reach a "self-awareness" age, when modesty becomes apparent. Think of the times when you have not received the attention you felt was appropriate. Have you ever offered your hand to someone who failed to shake it? Talked with someone who was not listening to you? Had someone hang up the telephone on you while you were talking? Experienced someone talking right through what you were saying? Had a waiter or clerk ignore you when you wanted service? All of these relationships are characterized by the lack of responsiveness of one party. Did you ever talk to someone who wouldn't, or couldn't, make eye contact? Have someone laugh at you when you didn't mean to be funny? Or have someone fail to laugh when you *did* mean to be funny? Experience another driver who ignored your signal or your horn? Who cut you off or rudely blocked your way? We are extremely sensitive to such "insults."

Too high a degree of responsiveness is equally disconcerting. No one likes to be stared at. Try getting on an elevator and, instead of turning around to face the door, remain with your back to it facing all of the other passengers. Look at each one in turn and smile at them. Most of them will become extremely uncomfortable and go to great lengths to try to ignore you. And you may find that it takes considerable effort on your part to continue looking at them. Many people tell me they dread standing up in front of others to give a presentation. It is perfectly understandable. That is one of the very few times in your life when every eye in the room is on you. Everywhere you look, others are responding to you intently. Your own wedding is another such event, equally unnerving for many.

How do you feel when you are approached by a salesperson who hovers around you trying too hard to please? Or toward someone of the opposite sex who is too attentive? Or of the same sex? Too much attention is every bit as uncomfortable as too little. Many city dwellers are annoyed by the intrusion of the noise of automobile burglar alarms that seem to go off at all hours without apparent provocation. I know quite a few who think, because people walk past screaming alarms and don't even look up, that such alarms don't work. But they do. They work on the sensitivity to responsiveness of the perpetrator of the crime. The very last thing anyone who is actually breaking into a car wants is a loud and persistent noise that attracts (or might possibly attract) attention (that is, a higher degree of responsiveness) to this illegal activity.

I have used extremes here to illustrate the fact that we are indeed responsive to the amount of attention that is paid to us or denied us. We are sensitive to it in very fine and subtle degrees. And nearly all of them are communicated nonverbally. Every culture is sensitive to degrees of interpersonal responsiveness. The acceptable standard will vary from culture to culture, but all cultures have such standards. If you sell to prospects in a particular culture, learn their responsive patterns and reflect them. They will respond more easily to you, and the right relationship will become possible because you have made it possible for them to relate comfortably to you.

In our North American culture, comfortable responsiveness is indicated through steady (but not intense) eye contact, active listening (which we will discuss in detail in Chapter 7), attentive posture (leaning in toward the other), agreeing gestures (chin stroking and nodding of the head), appropriate agreeing sounds ("uh-huh," "yes," "go on," laughter), intelligent questions, taking notes, and appropriate responding behavior (for example, obedience, directing, courtesy, smiles).

Authority

North Americans are strange creatures. We do not want to be pushed or bossed around; yet, at the same time, we detest wimpiness. We do not want our affairs handled by uncertain, apologetic Milquetoasts. We admire and respect strong assertive behavior. Many even respect aggressive behavior, though few want to be aggressed against. On the whole, however, most of us accept authority with relative ease.

Ask yourself how you would feel if your doctor apologized—after the operation! Has your lawyer ever apologized for making a mistake? If you have ever fought a traffic ticket in court and won, does the officer who issued it come over and apologize? Let's face it, when we board an airplane, a train, a bus, or even a taxi, we expect the pilot or driver to know where they are going, how to get there, and how to operate the craft they are in charge of. We become very uneasy when we suspect that they don't.

Authority is not merely a matter of unapologetic behavior either. Would you frequent a dentist who seemed uncomfortable with the drill or who hesitated in using the needle? I once took my car to a garage for repair and found the mechanic so ignorant with regard to my car that I had to drive away without the repair. He was so unsure of himself that I didn't dare to leave something I valued with him. Few of us enjoy being bowed and scraped to, and even fewer like to bow and scrape to others. Yet in Japan, where bowing is a major part of social ritual, reading and responding correctly to levels of authority conveyed through subtle gestures is a highly admired and most necessary art.

Americans generally want at least to appear to each other as equals. We want to get on a first-name basis early in the relationship. We tend to sit expansively in relaxed postures. We will often talk easily with complete strangers of our personal feelings or problems. We like to keep even our business contacts on an informal footing. Yet, within this studied casualness, there are a number of status messages that we read and respond to. We give more physical space to those we perceive to have a greater degree of authority than we have. Thus the boss's desk, chair, office, car, and home tend to be larger than those of his or her subordinates. Many a young executive on the way up has learned the hard way that it doesn't pay to own a fancier car than the boss's.

Precedent carries tremendous authority. How often have you heard unacceptable work or inadequate performance justified by the remark, "Well, that's the way we do things around here"? It's a strong argument to beat because even bad habits carry a lot of authority. Ask anyone who has ever quit smoking. We also show respect toward and admire people with special skills or knowledge, such as professional athletes, doctors, educators and authors. In addition, the old saying, "Clothes make the man," still applies, enlarged of course to include women. Uniforms command a response. Dark blue or black, plain or pinstriped suits are "power" uniforms in business.

The list could go on and on. My point here is merely to underline the fact that we constantly respond to both positive and negative authority messages without really thinking about exactly what it is that is influencing us. Therefore, in order to succeed in establishing a comfortable relationship with the prospect, the sales representative must project positive authority messages, most particularly in the first few moments of the first call. And he or she cannot afford to undermine the initial authority projected by conveying weak or wimpy messages later on in the sales cycle. The three strongest authority messages a salesperson can project are:

(1) asking solid open-ended questions and listening and responding consultatively to the answers; (2) having asked or
answered a question, remaining silent so that the customer
can think and decide on a response; and (3) confronting
problems, like objections, or concerns, or reality, with frank-
ness and confidence and without resorting to game playing,
defensiveness, or "sneaky slick tricks."

Time after time, as a trainer, as a manager, or as a
customer, I hear salespeople launch into techno-babble in
response to an objection. They trot out all of the features and
advantages they are selling and throw them at the poor
prospect to show that they really know their stuff. And then
they wonder why they fail to get that prospect to make a
commitment to buy from them. But what are customers
thinking at this point? They know when the salesperson
starts to try to dazzle them with technical jargon that they
have just won the win/lose "who's got the upper hand here?"
battle. The seller is on the defensive and digging like mad to
maneuver around the point the customer brought up. The
customer wins and the salesperson loses the right, the necessary authority, to ask him for, and to expect him to keep, a
commitment. But selling is a win/win game, so by winning at
the expense of the seller customers lose too. They lose the
opportunity to truly find out about what is being sold. They
lose the opportunity to satisfy their buying need with a
mutual exchange. They lose by ending the dialogue that leads
to the discovery of how the product or service can benefit
them. They lose by having to continue somewhere else their
search for whatever it is that they need. And they lose by
furthering the suspicion-filled win/lose attitude toward selling.

What happens, on the other hand, if the salesperson,
instead of plunging into a sea of features and advantages,
continues the dialogue by asking more questions, waiting
comfortably for the answers, and directing his or her com-
ments solely toward solving the customer's problems, toward
the benefits the customer seeks in making the purchase? The
balance is maintained. Equal to equal, they work toward a
mutual satisfaction of their needs. It is a win/win solution. If

customers are asked at this moment for a commitment, they will make it, and keep it, because they will feel comfortable with the relationship they have established with the seller. They will feel a sense of respect for that salesperson's expertise and ability to inspire confidence and to satisfy their needs.

Authority is simple. We look up to and respect those who are confident, unruffled, and nondefensive. We are made uncomfortable by behavior that shows a lack of confidence, any sign of desperation or anxiety, or that appears defensive or obsequious to us. This is why I emphasize that in framing their objectives salespeople must take the time to make themselves thoroughly comfortable with asking for the order, thoroughly justified in working toward that objective.

Affect

Of the three messages, this is probably the one that needs the least explanation. Affect, as I've said, is a fancy word for emotion, and we all know that it is better to sell while feeling "up" than "down." Nobody wants to buy from a sad sack. All of us enjoy being with people who are cheerful and happy. However, the happiness must be genuine. A false note makes the entire situation ring untrue and undermines all sales credibility. No one enjoys being subjected to a "glad hander" who slickly and glibly creates artificial bonhomie as a matter of routine.

The true value of being up is that it inspires others to respond in kind. I tell salespeople who work on the telephone that they must smile, not to feel better, not just because it sounds good over the phone, but because, when potential customers hear that smile on the phone they tend to smile back. Happiness breeds happy and positive responses.

Finally, as we'll see in Chapter 8, emotion is one of the crucial elements in persuasion. All of the rationalization and justification in the world won't persuade me to buy something if I don't "feel" right about it. I suspect it is the same for you too. I'm not talking here about projecting insane jollity. However, the customer must sense that the salesperson believes in what he or she is selling, feels positive about it, enjoys the interaction and social side of the job, and, in fact, likes doing it. Anything less inspires distrust and undermines the salesperson's authority.

Language and Relationships

I have mentioned that most of the behavior that creates strong relationships is completely transparent to us. We give off impressions and read and respond to those given off by others without really thinking about them. They happen at a level below our conscious focus of attention. We can make ourselves aware of them, but unless we make a conscious effort to do so, we normally won't. Among the subtlest and most powerful of these unnoticed behaviors is our choice of words, the very language we use.

Test yourself. Read the following dialogue and then stop. Don't read my analysis of it until you've tried to zero in on the implications of the language each of the two speakers is using. Both use metaphors that reveal where they are coming from; that is, the metaphors reveal a situation other than the one the speakers are actually in that they unconsciously think of as very much like the one they are in and so they use language that describes that other, different situation to talk about the real one. See if you can spot the main metaphors at play in this dialogue:

Customer: I'm really locked in on this year's budget, Fred. My hands are tied. There's absolutely nothing I can do to move ahead. There's simply no way out of the position we're committed to. You ask me to buy your service, and I'd like to, but I'm just not free to make that move.

Sales rep: But if you could just pitch to your boss, Marty, that the services we're offering you here would allow you to knock your competition right out of the ballpark, I'm sure you could get to first base with him.

Customer: No. I'm just helpless to change the facts. I really would like to come along. I'd love to be free of these budgetary restraints, but I'm really locked in. They're watching this department like a hawk. I can't move without coming under the gun. There's just no way I can get the message through to the boss. I'm sold, but I just can't get out of the spot I'm in. I'm chained to it, locked in tight.

Sales rep: Marty, you don't have to try for a home run with this thing. All we need is to get to first base. Once I get a chance to field his objections we can bring the whole package home. You'll get a run up on the competition and I'll score a major sale. But first, we've got to be able to pitch the deal to your boss.

Stop reading. What are the metaphors being used by each player?

Okay, how did you do? Did you pick out the dominant phrases in Marty's conversation as "locked in," "hands are tied," "nothing I can do to move ahead," "no way out," "committed," "not free to make that move," "helpless," "like to come along," "love to be free of . . . restraints," "they're watching [me] like a hawk," "I can't move without coming under the gun," "no way [to] get the message through," "I . . . can't get out of the spot I'm in," "I'm chained to it, locked in tight"? If you take all of these phrases together, what do they describe? The life of a prisoner! If you ask him, of course Marty wouldn't say, "Oh, I'm in jail!" Yet unconsciously, when he feels this kind of pressure, he uses language that sounds *as if* he were in jail to express his frustration and, in doing so, reveals a great deal about his attitude and feelings.

Let's look at Fred's language. Did you select "pitch," "knock . . . out of the ballpark," "get to first base," "try for a home run," "field . . . objections," "bring . . . home," "get a run up," "score"? This one's easier, isn't it? Fred's out there playing baseball. Even though this dialogue is a bit exaggerated, we have all heard people use such metaphors. They are real. And, in this situation, are these two men talking to each other? Will either resolve his concerns through this conversation? Of course not. Fred's out in "left field" playing ball while Marty's locked up in a jail and wishing he could get out. There is absolutely no communication going on here—and nothing but a poor and resentful relationship being built. Fred will never sell Marty his services as long as he continues to talk baseball while Marty "can't play ball."

We've all heard the expression "Now you're talking my language." It means "I'm responding to what you are saying. It appeals to me. You are reaching me. I like what you are saying and I understand it." Wouldn't we all like our prospects to say this to us? Of course we would. It says that we have established the right relationship and that the prospect wants to buy from us because he sees us as someone like himself, as someone who talks his language. One of the surest ways to gain credibility, authority, and the right relationship is to enter into the metaphors the prospect uses and to use them yourself.

Stop reading. Take a moment to think how Fred might have done so in the dialogue.

If Fred shifts to Marty's prison metaphor, he can get a lot further with him. If he offers "the key" to help him "break out of the bind he's in," "overcome the barrier" of the competition, "get out from under the gun" of a "tight" budget, "loosen the constraints," "burst free" into the marketplace, he still may not make a sale (after all, there are no guarantees) but he'll have reached Marty, spoken to his condition, and if Marty ever gets a budget, he's definitely going to buy from Fred.

Spotting people's main metaphors can be difficult and it takes practice, lots of practice. Try it out on your family at home, on business associates and friends, and then on customers. You can make yourself very adept at this skill, and it will pay off with easier, faster, closer sales relationships with customers.

There is, however, yet another way of talking the customer's language, a way many people feel is easier to adopt than getting inside a metaphor. Each of us tends habitually to depend more on one of our senses than on the others to tell us about the world we live in. Some people are more likely to trust information if they can see it, others if they can hear it, and still others if they can touch it or feel it. Each of us builds up a way of absorbing the world from very early childhood on. Do you believe more readily what you see in print or what you hear from someone you trust? Do you believe it's going to rain because you read the forecast in the newspaper, because you heard the weatherman on TV say it would, or because your arthritis acted up this morning and that always means rain no matter what the media say?

I was recently talking with a friend who told me he was very concerned because he found himself completely unmoved by the controversy over whether the act of burning the American flag should be classified as illegal or as a basic freedom of speech. I was surprised because this was a very patriotic fellow, someone who really cared, who, as he explained to me, was often moved to tears by hearing the national anthem. But he was completely unmoved when he saw a flag burned or, for that matter, when he saw one waving in the breeze. He was puzzled and distressed by this and asked me if I had run into any kind of explanation that would set his mind at ease.

I told him about the sensory biases we all have. It was like a revelation to him. As we talked, it became clear that instance after instance of his everyday behavior was aurally (hearing) biased. Practically everything he did or cared about was related in some way to speech or sound, and very little to what was visual or written or tactile, despite the fact that he holds advanced academic degrees and was at the time the president of the academic senate of a major university. It didn't matter what was written; it was what people said that held interest for him. What he saw (like a flag burning on television) had far less impact on him than what he heard (for instance, the national anthem). He was, and had always been, an exceptionally aural person.

Each of us relates to the world through one of four sensory biases. It doesn't really matter whether we are visually oriented (as I am), aurally (hearing) oriented (as my friend is), kinesthetically (touch) oriented, or empathically (feelings) oriented. What matters is that we reveal which of these ways of looking at the world (notice my visual bias here) we have adopted by the way we describe things, by the language we use. Here are a few common expressions that salespeople hear quite frequently. I've italicized the words that reveal the speaker's bias:

- No matter which way I *look* at it, I don't *see* where we're really going to benefit by . . .
- I *hear* what you're *saying*.
- I'm *sure* my boss (family, husband, and so on) won't *like* it.
- It *looks good* and I can *see* where we might be able to use it in a year or so, but it just doesn't *look* like something we need right now.
- I just don't *feel right* about *dropping* our present supplier.
- The way I *hear* it you're *promising* something you won't be able to deliver.
- I want *something real, something I can get my teeth into* that will do what I want done, not just some "pie-in-the-sky" promise.

If you listen for the sensory bias of your prospects and customers, you can quickly and easily adjust your language to enter into theirs and "see, hear, or feel" things as they do.

In this chapter we've looked at a number of behavioral concepts that play a powerful role in the "partnering" process that must take place between a sales representative and a customer. I constantly run into salespeople who worry that such ideas are too "soft," that they are not sufficiently "hands on" (note the tactile bias) to be useful. If you are one such reader, let me share with you that it is my experience from years of selling and from training thousands of salespeople in these concepts and the skills to practice them that they really do work. By consciously creating relationships with prospects and customers that are nonzero/sum, that demonstrate high responsiveness, affect, and firm authority, both in manner and in preparation, you will improve your selling. By consciously creating relationships that are based on the recognition, analysis, and understanding of the roles that each of you is playing for the other, and on the power of a sound relationship to overwhelm any content, you will improve your closing ratio. By creating relationships that flow from an observation and astute analysis of the nonverbal and linguistic behavior employed by both the customer and the seller, you will increase your ability to develop new customers with relative ease. This is so because practicing all of these skills will allow you to align your sales efforts with your customers' need to buy, and of course when you do this they will buy from you.

7

Questions:
The Art of Selling

Whoever asks questions controls the conversation. This is so whether we are face to face with friends or strangers, on the telephone, conducting business, or providing constructive feedback to our offspring. Sometimes people will argue with me on this point, saying, "Not so! If I am well prepared and have planned what I'm going to say, while I'm saying it I am in full control. I know what I will say next, I know what I am saying now. I am in control." All I have to do to prove them wrong is to interrupt them by asking a question! If I say something like, "Excuse me, but what do you mean exactly when you say 'prepared?'" they now have to break their prepared flow in order to digress into the realm of definitions that I have introduced. If I keep on asking questions, I can pull them so far off track that they may never get back on. I take control when I ask the question.

What's Wrong (and Right) With Questions

In my customer service seminars one problem comes up frequently. How do you control the upset customer on the telephone who simply will not stop talking, will not let you get a word in edgewise? My answer is simple. Ask an irrelevant question. I always use the fictitious name Carpenter.

"Excuse me, is this about the Carpenter account?" I'll inquire.

"The what?" says the talkative customer invariably.

"The Carpenter account," I repeat.

"No," says the customer, "of course not. It's about *my* account."

"Oh," I reply, having now wrested full control of the call from the talkative one, "then what you have to do is . . ."

If you have any doubt about this technique, try it yourself. The next time someone who is upset calls you about something, interrupt the flow of complaints by asking if it's about Carpenter (or whatever name you'd prefer) and see how immediately you bring the complainer to a puzzled halt from which you can easily take control of the call. Or, as an alternative, the next time someone telephones you and proceeds to read a mechanical script to you, simply interrupt and ask a question. As soon as your caller goes back to the script, interrupt again and ask another question. By continually wresting the topic of conversation away from such people and preventing them from completing the script you will gain complete control of the call. But if you do this, remember that they are salespeople too and you have just made their jobs a great deal more difficult. They may deserve a sale for the extra effort you have forced them to expend.

Of course, if they are skilled, they will answer your question and end their reply with a question back to you that puts them right onto their script again. If they do that, answer their question and end your answer with another question back to them. After three or four such volleys they will beg you to get off the phone. They have a quota of something like thirty calls per hour to meet and they don't have time for power games.

Asking questions, however, requires great care because questions can (and often do) create hostility and resistance rather than openness and trust. The kinds of questions you ask and the sequence in which you ask them govern your customer's responses. You can create a warm and productive relationship with questions, or a cool and suspicious one. Fortunately, the art of asking questions is a prime selling skill available to anyone who will take it seriously and who will practice diligently. It is always surprising to me that so many of the salespeople I meet don't bother to develop the art of framing questions. All lawyers know the importance of it and carefully craft their cross-examinations. All representatives in Congress who sit on a commission that holds hearings know the importance of it and set their staff people to long nighttime hours carefully preparing and framing the questions to be asked at the next day's hearings. Yet many salespeople look upon questions as something spontaneous, as something that can be asked off the top of the head, willy-nilly, inspirationally. And they are wrong! Questions are the most potent selling tool there is and deserve the careful attention that pays off in more effective sales.

Question Formats

There are two types of questions: open-ended and closed-ended. An open-ended question is one that can be answered freely in whatever way the one being asked chooses. The answer may stray off the topic, be long-winded or short. It is whatever the one being questioned wants to say about what was asked. A closed-ended question, by contrast, has a specific answer that is often anticipated by the questioner. The answer to it is limited to a narrow range of choices. Many times the answer is either yes or no.

Of these two types of questions, which do you think is most commonly used in the sales interview situation? If you picked closed-ended as the most common form, you'd be right. Yet when we ask nothing but closed-ended "probes" we create an adversary, not a customer. For instance, how would you feel if you were asked to answer the following questions?

- What is your name?
- What is your Social Security number?
- What is your telephone number?
- What is your address?

- How long have you lived at this address?
- Where did you live before?
- How much do you pay for your mortgage (rent)?
- Are you married?
- To whom?
- What is your spouse's Social Security number?

Pretty intrusive, aren't they? And boring. You'd probably be annoyed and perhaps even offended at having to waste your time answering such questions.

On the other hand, what happens if I say to you, "Tell me about yourself"? Stop reading for a moment and think of an answer. Got one? Okay, now, how did you feel while you were thinking up how to answer such a question? I'll bet your mind strolled over some pleasant details of your life, became engaged in thinking what you could comfortably reveal and what you couldn't, or wandered off into some particularly interesting side thought. Even if you were impatient with the question, you approached it as something you were responsible for answering.

It is this sense of personal responsibility that makes open-ended questions so much more effective than closed-ended ones in helping customers to disclose their buying patterns and needs. A closed-ended question puts pressure on the person questioned to answer, but that person blames the one who asked it. It builds resentment toward the asker. An open-ended question, however, actually puts more pressure on people to answer, but they take on the responsibility for answering and don't build resistance toward the one who asked it. So when I say, "How are you presently handling this situation?" or, "What do you look for when you buy xyz?" I am much more likely to get informative answers than if I were to ask, "Is that an xyz machine?" or, "Who did you buy that from?"

The advantages of open-ended questions over closed-ended ones for building relationships with prospects become apparent. But why, then, do so many salespersons insist on "probing" customers in the face of their well-known resentment of it? One reason I've already alluded to: Salespeople, for the most part, seem to take asking questions for granted and don't practice to refine the skill. They tend to want to take the easy way and simply do what comes naturally. And closed-ended questions seem more natural because they are the ones we have most often been asked throughout our lives. What were the most common forms of tests and quizzes in school? Short answer, multiple choice, true/false—all closed-ended. What was the one open-ended format? Essays, but how often did we have to write them? And when we came home from school, what did our parents ask? "What did you learn at school today?" or, "Where have you been?" or, "Who are you going to be with?" or, "What are you doing?" Again, all closed-ended! We also ask closed-ended questions because they are easier to think of and because they elicit information that we can predict and structure, and they allow us to control the flow of information from the prospect. Unfortunately, the prospect usually feels that control and resists it.

I should state clearly here that despite all of these negatives, there is nothing wrong with closed-ended questions in and of themselves. It is the overreliance on them that is the problem. Of course we still need the specific information they provide. But if we line them up and fire them off with machine-gunlike precision as if we were conducting an interrogation, we hurt our sales effort and fail to align it with the prospect's need to buy. I recommend a careful blending of the two formats. Ask open-ended questions to start with and then begin to zero in and clarify with closed-ended ones. Watch for any tension or the beginnings of reluctance to answer and, at that point, ask another open-ended one. When the prospect relaxes, you can go back to closed-ended questions as needed.

The catch is that most people have trouble thinking of open-ended questions off the top of their heads. The solution is to write down six or so carefully phrased open-ended questions, developed during your leisure, before you make the sales call. Keep them handy during the call so that when you want to ease the pressure on the prospect you can simply refer to your list and find the next open-ended question. If you sold industrial chemicals, for instance, your open-ended list might look something like this:

1. What do you look for in a vendor of raw chemicals?
2. What has been your experience with your present suppliers?
3. What do you like best/least about the service you get now?
4. What is the most important thing (service) a chemicals vendor can do for you?
5. Where do you anticipate the raw chemicals market will be headed in the next six months?
6. How would I go about becoming one of your suppliers in that scenario?

With a list like this to guide you, you can ask a series of specific closed-ended questions and then, if the prospect seems a bit reluctant, ask him or her the first open one on your list. Follow it up with specific closed-ended ones if you need to, or open the prospect up even more by asking the second one. If you ask all six, you'll gather a lot of useful information, build a deeper relationship, and probably have ample opportunity for closed-ended follow-up questions after each open-ended one.

Steps to Improving Questioning Skills

There are three steps you can take to refine your questioning skills. The first is to gain a comfort level in framing open-ended questions. As I've just indicated, it's not easy to stop thinking in closed-ended formats. Start by writing down all of the questions you would normally ask a prospect or customer. You must actually write them down. Psychologists claim that anything you keep in your head is only an idea. If you write it down you can look at it, judge it, see it objectively. So long as it is only in your head, you will see it subjectively, with bias. Get it out into the real world. Examine each question and try to rephrase it into an open-ended format. If it is already open-ended, rephrase it as a different open-ended one. This is good practice. Ask family members or friends to join you and come up with their own phrasings. The object is to become perfectly relaxed in asking for any information you need using either an open- or a closed-ended format.

The second step is to take the time after each sales call to sit down privately, stay in your car, and go over the entire dialogue you have just had with that customer while it is still fresh in your mind. As you do so, write down in a notebook every question you asked. Underline the closed-ended ones. For every closed-ended question, once again, figure out a way to ask the same thing in an open-ended format. For instance, in the chemical sales example, suppose you asked, "How big an order do you normally place?" The same information (and a lot more of it) would come if you said instead, "You have a huge operation here. How do you cycle orders to anticipate the demand of each process so as not to fall short on supply?" Or, if you sold home safety alarms and you had asked, "Do you have an alarm system right now?" you might rephrase that question into something more like, "What has been your experience with alarm systems in the past?" or, "How has neighborhood safety changed in the last year or so from when you first moved in?" Once you have an open-ended framework, write down the new question. Save the list and date it each day. As the closed-ended list grows shorter and the open-ended one grows longer, date it each week. In this way you can monitor your improvement. Repeat these steps until asking open-ended questions becomes second nature for you.

As the third step, I recommend that you play the Question Game. It is a skill game and here's how to play it. Whenever you are with someone, preferably not a customer at first, try to see how long you can keep that person talking without having to say anything yourself other than asking questions. If you have to answer a question yourself, or respond with anything other than a question, your time has run out. You have to start over again. Play the game every chance you get. It is particularly effective (and challenging) with hotel desk clerks, waiters and waitresses, cab drivers, and people who sit next to you on airplanes.

What you will learn from this game is what I call the "question reflex." You will become so adept at asking questions that whenever anything happens, whenever a customer raises an objection, changes tactics, or does something you didn't expect, your first reaction will be to ask questions. If you are challenged, instead of rising to the challenge right away, you will first deflate it and put it in perspective with a question. If customers become upset with you, instead of becoming defensive or indulging in an angry outburst, you will ask a question. This technique gives you power. Remember, the one who asks questions controls the conversation. The question game reinforces the question reflex, which in turn gives you leverage in any selling situation.

You can practice the question game with anyone. People won't mind. In fact they will appreciate it. I have a friend named Neil who is the finest question asker I know. He plays this game all the time. I've asked many of his customers and colleagues why they like to talk with Neil. The answer is always the same: "Because he is such a great conversationalist"!

How to Use Questions

According to the world-famous negotiator Gerard Nierenberg, there are only five functions or uses for questions.[1] You can use a question to gain attention, to get information, to give information, to direct the thought of others, and to close. Let's look at each one of these functions.

Many of us use questions *to gain attention or to focus it* on a particular aspect of our communication. Questions like "May I just point out . . . ?" or "Can you help me?" or "Did you notice the smoothness of the downshift?" or "Can you see clearly?" all fit into this category. Notice that they are usually closed-ended. They are highly controlling questions that direct the customer's attention to wherever you want it to be.

The *getting information function* is the one we most readily think of when someone asks what we use questions for. Questions such as, "How are you presently handling this

[1]Gerard Nierenberg, *The Complete Negotiator* (New York: Nierenberg & Zeif, 1986), pp. 101–127.

situation?" or, "Have you ever used our product (service) in the past?" or, "How did we perform for you then?" or, "How should I proceed?" are all in this category. Notice again that some of these questions are closed-ended, though it is common to find an open-ended one or two.

The *giving information* question is very tricky to use because it can easily imply superiority on the part of the person asking it. The last thing you want is to sound condescending to your prospect. On the other hand, used infrequently and with care, this type of question can focus attention and arouse interest very effectively. Questions such as, "Did you know that our service has just won the national honors award?" or, "Have you read where ABC company is about to declare bankruptcy?" or, "Are you familiar with our new xyz services?" all provide information and, at the same time, open up a discussion or create focus. If they are indeed news to the prospect, they can be very effective in building interest for you. But use them with care.

The fourth category, *causing the customer to think,* is my personal favorite. In fact, unless I watch myself, I tend to overuse it. This format is the most open-ended of them all. It is best used as a way of dealing with objections or of involving customers in creative brainstorming for a solution to their problems. Questions such as, "Why?" or, "What aspects of your current service seem to work best for you?" or, "What do you look for when you buy an xyz?" or, "I'll bet there's a fascinating story behind what you just said. Will you tell it to me, please?" or, "What is your response to that?" all make the customer think. And a thinking customer is involved in building a relationship and seeing benefits, not in shutting you out and saying "no."

Nierenberg's final category, *closing,* is a powerful, effective, and easy use of questions. Good closing questions can range from something as simple as, "So, where do we go from here?" to the classic sharp-angle close, "If I can get it in xyz, will you buy it now?" Part of the reason is that though they are not manipulative they are the logical assertive next step when the salesperson has finished presenting a solution to the customer's problem. In effect, when you close with a question, you are asking the customer, "Are you ready to close?" The customer's answer is the answer to your selling objective and the purpose of your call. Customers will buy when they are ready. Salespeople must learn to ask when they are ready in order to allow them to buy. We'll look more intensely at using questions to close when we talk about handling objections and closing in Chapters 9 and 10.

Why Do We Need to Ask Questions Anyway?

If customers aren't sold but rather buy when they are ready, then isn't selling relegated to simple order taking? And, if that is so, what is the point of asking any questions other than, "Are you ready yet?" This is a reasonable, logical question. Let me answer it by saying that not only is it important to ask questions; questions are actually the single most important part of the sales interaction. Here's why.

As I have said all along, customers buy when they are ready. The problem is that many people simply do not know when they are ready. I once had a fellow in a "training the sales trainer" seminar. He wanted to become a sales trainer. At the end of the training, in his evaluation of the course he stated that there was very little in it that was new to him. I knew that what I was teaching was the state of the art and so I went to him to ask why he felt that nothing was new. He told me that mine was the fourth "training the sales trainer" course he'd taken and that I'd covered the same things he'd already learned.

"If you've taken three other courses in the same subject, why on earth did you take mine?" I asked in amazement.

"I just felt I'd be better prepared with one more," he replied.

What he had needed was not another course but, rather, someone to sell him on his own ability and readiness to be a sales trainer.

Frequently we remain unaware of our needs. Sometimes we know the business or interpersonal need we seek to satisfy without being at all aware of the personal inner needs we are striving to satisfy or of the constituent ones that may be pressuring us. The task then facing a skilled salesperson is first to select prospects who are likely to be ready to buy, then to create a relationship of mutual trust with those prospects so that they will not feel threatened by the salesperson, then to examine through low-pressure questions the degree of each prospect's readiness to buy and the needs at play that make for that readiness, and finally to bring those needs into the prospects' conscious awareness so that they will recognize their own readiness to buy and will satisfy it with the salesperson's product or service. If they are indeed ready, they will buy. "Selling" occurs when the salesperson creates the relationship, draws out the needs, examines them, demonstrates them to the customer, and asks for the order.

Needs

Questions are the tool we use to explore the need, the readiness of our customers to buy. This is what makes them the essence of effective selling. Once you ask the "right" questions, you discover the need to buy and either wait for a better time if the prospect isn't ready yet or present to that need if he or she is ready. The actual questions we ask necessarily vary from customer to customer, from product to service, from salesperson to salesperson. But in order to know what questions to ask and what to look for in the answers we receive we must look at the subject of needs, in particular three theories that seem to best explain how they motivate us. Let's look briefly at some of the conclusions drawn from their research into motivation by Kurt Lewin[2], Abraham Maslow[3], and Frederick Hertzberg[4]. First, we'll examine the general theory of each, and then we'll look at how these theories can help us to frame and use questions to help our customers to buy.

Kurt Lewin was a social psychologist. He was hired dur-

[2]Kurt Lewin, *Field Theory in Social Science,* ed. D. Cartwright (New York: Harper & Row, 1951).
[3]Abraham Maslow, *Motivation and Personality* (New York: Harper & Row, 1954).
[4]Frederick Hertzberg, *Work and the Nature of Man* (New York: World, 1966).

ing World War II to try to sell Americans on the idea of eating processed meat (Spam). He traveled around the United States holding Spam rallies to sell people on the merits of inexpensive processed meats. In doing so, he also learned a great deal about what convinces people and what doesn't.

Lewin theorized that human beings are forced into making decisions by their own personal desire for one of two totally opposed and mutually exclusive goals: maintaining the status quo, or making some sort of change in that status quo. All of the reasons for maintaining the status quo pull us in one direction. All of the reasons for changing our state pull us in the opposite direction. These two opposing forces create a "force field" in which we can be influenced by adding forces to one side and/or by removing forces from the other. We are always constantly pulled in these opposite directions—staying the same or changing—and we are consequently trying to create a balance between the two:

CHANGE———< ——< —< **SELF**——> ——> ——> **STATUS QUO**

Each new state of equilibrium (balance) is only temporary, but always feels more or less permanent because we have achieved it by actively balancing our opposing desires. Such states of "quasi-stationary equilibrium," as Lewin called them, are reached by making decisions. Making decisions thus provides a sense of relief from the tension created by the opposing forces in the field. Recognizing that this two-way pull is always at play in the mind-set of the prospect and responding to it appropriately is one of the keys to effective selling. By anticipating and then correctly reading the opposing forces at play the salesperson can influence the customer and help to relieve the discomfort felt by bringing that customer into a feeling of balance, through making a decision.

To illustrate Lewin's force field in action, take a moment to notice whether or not you are fully comfortable as you sit reading this book. Notice how you are sitting, how long you have been in one position, where each of your limbs is placed, and so on. Concentrate on one limb, say your left foot. Now, as you think about it, decide whether or not you want to move it to a different position. Weigh your desire to stay where you are versus your desire to move. You will either want to move the foot or want to keep it where it is. One direction will definitely outweigh the other. If it doesn't, you will feel frustration and tension until you decide either to move or to stay put. When you do either one, you will feel relief. The more uptight you were over the move (or nonmove), the more relief you will feel. It is this sense of relief that you bring to your customers when you help them to relieve the tension between their need to buy versus their desire not to be sold. You are helping them to restore the balance.

"Aha!" you say. "I know my own limbs and can argue with myself about whether or not to move them, but how can I tell where my customer is in such a force field?" You do so by asking questions; by recognizing and responding appropriately to the roles and arenas your prospect is operating in; and by gaining credibility through the predictability principle. You do so by making presentations that add to your side of the balance, as will be discussed in Chapter 8, by responding persuasively to objections, as we shall see in Chapter 9, and by clarifying the decision for the prospect, as we shall do in Chapter 10.

Abraham Maslow, a contemporary of Lewin, took this concept a step further. He felt that the multitude of human needs and desires could be classified into categories. In Maslow's view, we are always involved in a balance of opposing needs that operate in a constant cycle. The needs create desires on which we act. Our actions then produce consequences that affect our needs either positively or negatively. These in turn create new desires and new actions, and so forth. Thus, an unsatisfied need would create tension, either pleasant or unpleasant, and it would energize and motivate the individual's behavior.

But we don't respond with equal energy to all of our needs. Obviously some needs appear to be more important, or at least more powerful, than others in influencing our behavior. So Maslow hit upon the concept of arranging the needs that drive our behavior in a hierarchy of ascending power based on their ability to affect our behavior (Figure 7-1). At

Figure 7-1. Maslow's hierarchy of needs.

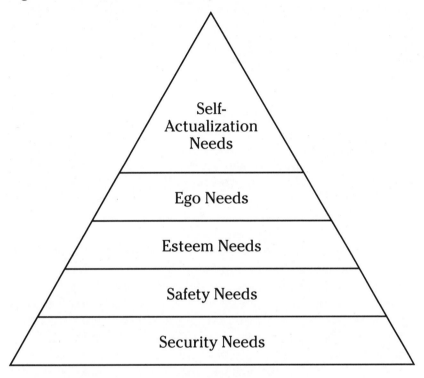

the very bottom of the pyramid, its base, is our need for survival, or security. It is the most powerful because when it is threatened everything else takes a back seat to satisfying it by eliminating whatever threatens us.

Into this category Maslow placed our physiological needs—our need for food, shelter, sense of security, and so forth. If whatever you are selling is perceived by the prospect as threatening his or her security (job, salary, values, comfortable routine), you will trigger a response from this need level. It is extremely powerful and so must be dealt with immediately. Thus if you are selling electronic hardware that can be perceived as threatening to take away jobs or to change work flow, you most likely will have to prepare for strong resistance. It was the disturbing of this deep physiological need, you will remember, that got Lloyd Dickerson thrown out of Wright's office. This is why it is vital to build trust with your prospect. This is also why it is vital to time your sales call to the buying cycles of your prospects so that what you are doing falls into place as part of the routine that they are currently following.

The second most powerful level is safety needs. These are very closely related to security needs and both are extremely powerful motivators of behavior. The only real distinction between them is that most of us will risk our safety in order to satisfy our security needs. Thus the primitive tribal hunter risks his life daily in order to find and kill food for his family, and for much the same reason modern workers undergo stressful commutes that subject them to traffic and crime risks on their way to workplaces that are fraught with further stress and that frequently force them to breathe unhealthy air. The biological needs outweigh the safety needs. This is why you must always place a high priority on making your customers look good to their constituents. Currently I sell an intangible service, training, and most of my clients' jobs ride on the success of their decision to hire me. If what you sell causes your customers to take risks, then you and I are in the same boat. If what you are selling threatens your prospects' sense of safety, causes them to feel at risk politically in their organization, carries the potential for them to lose face or look silly in front of their peers or families, creates the risk of confrontation with others over the need for or the correctness of the purchase, you will be forced to deal with this deep and powerful need. Indeed this is the source of the dreaded "price" objection. If buying what you are selling risks some other, treasured part of the prospect's life, you will have to counter this need. If, on the other hand, you can ally yourself with this need, it can work in your favor.

Again linked to the level immediately below it in power, the third level is the social or esteem need. In this instance we are concerned with the judgment of others, with our interaction with them. We do not like to feel alone. If you are asking your prospect to be innovative, if you are selling the very latest quantum leap in technology, you will probably have to deal with this very powerful source of resistance. This level of needs also influences friendships, which is why it is always advisable to create as warm and friendly a relationship as possible with any prospect. It is also why the longer you persist in friendly calls at politely determined times, the more likely you are eventually to close a sale because the customer becomes comfortable with the relationship with you and begins to invest trust in you.

Above the social or esteem needs are the ego needs. It is not enough for us simply not to lose face; we must be well regarded as well. We need to hold our heads up with pride before our peers. This is why those with greater authority in companies tend to have more expensive perks. Does a key to the executive washroom really make a difference? You bet it does! What possible practical reason is there for purchasing a $165,000 Rolls Royce except to say, "I own one"? I agree that it is a wonderful car, but so is a Mercedes for less than half the price. And many other very fine automobiles are available for less than the Mercedes. One owns such items as status symbols to indicate a standing in the community of wealth. The motivation here is the need for ego satisfaction. Each of us needs to be well thought of both by others (the need to be loved) and by ourselves. We want to be proud of ourselves. Thus ethics can be an effective appeal. The greater the need or desire to feel comfortable ethically, the more powerful the feeling of motivation.

At the very pinnacle of Maslow's hierarchy is what he calls self-actualization needs. He describes this need as the motivation to satisfy personal goals, to be active and always moving in some direction. It is the source of personal curiosity, the need to know. It is why we love puzzles and stories and jokes, why we support a multibillion-dollar entertainment industry, and why professional sports has become such a huge industry worldwide. It is also why we diet and jog and play games with each other, why we have families and strive to see that our kids have the chance to "do better" than we did.

How does all this theory relate to selling to customers who want to buy? It relates in this way: Even the prospect who very much wants to buy that Rolls Royce will fail to do so if buying it would create too great a risk to safety or security. Both motivation and resistance come from these interrelated needs, and the more powerful ones—those found lower on the pyramid—nearly always triumph over those that are higher up. As an effective salesperson, you can relate and present your product or services to those lower and more powerful motivators or, if they speak normally to the higher ones, you can at least prepare for the resistance that will probably arise if the lower ones are excited by the desire of the prospect to buy.

Frederick Hertzberg was interested in discovering which factors in the work environment motivated and influenced workers. His concern was that most managers and investigators seemed to believe that wages, working conditions, job security, and company policy were the major considerations that moved workers to improve their performance. In much the same way, most of the salespeople I talk to in my seminars or coach in the field seem to be concerned almost exclusively with price as the major and most difficult objection they face. Even in my classes on negotiation, price frequently becomes the stumbling block, the barrier to better solutions.

Hertzberg wanted to discover if indeed people were turned on by such factors as wages and prices, so he set up a survey of worker attitudes. From this he discovered that money was not really what motivated people most deeply. Certainly people became upset over not having enough of it, or over paying too much of it, but only insofar as they perceived that someone else was getting a better deal. Hertzberg saw a parallel between our attitude toward money and how we look at cleanliness. We usually wash our hands only when they are dirty or as a matter of routine. Only a desire to be clean or to maintain regular habits motivates us hygienically. Believing that the same was true of money and working conditions, Hertzberg labeled such concerns "hygiene factors," things that motivate us only when they are *not* present or when they appear to be more in the possession of others.

A lack of what is perceived to be satisfactory will stimulate a response from the average worker. The same is frequently true of customers who raise price as an objection. It is not usually the money itself that motivates the price haggle, but rather the customer perception that someone else may be getting a discount or a better deal than what has been offered them. Those who sell luxury cars tell me that no one argues about the first $60,000 or $70,000, only about the last $1,500 or so.

If money isn't the big motivator, what is? Hertzberg's studies show that people are inspired to work harder or better by such things as a sense of achievement, recognition, responsibility exercised, the perception of the work as work, the possibility for personal growth, and the nature of the work itself. These things he labeled "satisfiers" because they were the factors that provided satisfaction, whereas the hygiene factors motivated only through the sense of dissatisfaction they created.

Stop reading for a moment and think of your hobby if you have one. If you don't, think of someone you know who jogs, or gardens, or engages regularly in some personal activities of this sort. Now ask yourself, "why do I (they) do it? At the end of a difficult or exhausting day, why do I (they) come home and indulge in yet more hard work?" For money? Job security? Policy? Working conditions? Of course not! People work at hobbies, often much harder than they ever work at their jobs, because doing so provides them with a sense of achievement and the possibility for growth. It provides them with recognition among other hobbyists, and it is fun, a joy and pleasure to perform, not work at all. They do it for all of Hertzberg's satisfier reasons and only marginally, if at all, for his hygienic ones.

How does this apply to selling? People buy things for much the same reasons. And our purpose here, remember, is to align our selling efforts with the prospect's buying urge. Anyone who has ever sold equipment to industry knows the pride the new owners invariably take in their state-of-the-art purchase, frequently even bragging about the huge sums they paid for it. Their purchase gives them a sense of achievement and recognition. Anyone who has ever sold services to industry or to individuals knows the sense of pride of ownership customers feel when they talk about "their" consultant, or decorator, furrier, accountant, or software or maintenance contract. They often measure their sense of success (progress) by whom they hire to serve them. They will still sometimes haggle over price because they think it is expected of them and because they don't want to feel that someone else got a better deal. But very few sales are made or lost on price alone unless the prospect really cannot afford the purchase. In such a case, the prospect should not have been selected as a viable candidate in the first place.

Because our discussion of needs arises out of our work on questions, we must now look at what kinds of questions you can use to estimate the needs at play in a given sales situation. The balance of forces in Lewin's model will usually be revealed by questions that summarize or project ahead to a time when the sale is closed. Such questions as, "Let's see, what have we decided so far?" or, "Do you see where this might pay off for you?" fit into this category. So do questions like, "What is the procedure now to move ahead with the order?" and, "Is there anything else that prevents us from making a deal tonight?" In the early qualifying stages of the sale you might ask, "How did you come to buy xyz?" or, a favorite of mine in a business-to-business sale, "What's your procedure for getting approval of such an order? What are the steps and who else needs to examine it?" Or even, "So what's the next step? Where do we go from here?"

Many of these questions will also reveal Maslow's social and esteem needs levels at play. The safety and security needs are rarer in sales situations, but they tend to be revealed by questions that force prospects to justify their objections. Saying, "You don't seem to be happy with my conclusion. May I ask you why not?" will usually cause a reaction that will reveal the deeper needs at play if there are any. So will statements that threaten to call an end to the negotiation like, "That's the best I can do. We go with it like this or I'll have to call the deal off. What do you say?" Self-actualization as a motive is revealed by offering to let the prospect move ahead by asking, "So, how should we preceed?" or, "What can

I do for you today?" or, "I can give you a little here, but I'd like a little in return. Can you make me look good?"

Finally, Hertzberg's satisfiers are often revealed by leading questions such as, "Doesn't it feel good when things work out right?" and, "That sounds like a frustrating call you just had, is it really rough?" Of course such questions can border on being too personal, and you'll have to be guided by your own comfort level in using them. My point here is that by asking such questions you will trigger responses from prospects or customers that will reveal their need state. Then, when the initial call is completed, in your assessment of it afterwards you can answer the following questions:

- What personal, corporate, and constituent factors work for me here?
- What ones work against me?
- Are there any homeostatic or security needs at play here that will work for or against me?
- What are the safety needs (if any) at play?
- Are there social needs that I can capitalize on or that will oppose the sale?
- What esteem needs could hinder the sale or help me to help this prospect make a decision?
- What are the self-actualization needs involved?
- What satisfiers can be brought into play to help this customer?

Remember that the goal in this exercise is not to manipulate but to look for those frequently unconscious needs that influence your prospects and, once you find the needs, to help the prospect to move toward a decision in your favor; or, if the needs are too strong, to recognize that the time is not right and to withdraw till your customer is ready to buy. Examining the needs at play lets you discover when the customer is ready to buy and in *need* of a decision. Asking questions uncovers those needs.

Resistance

When your questions uncover what appears to be resistance to your sales efforts, remember that the problem most likely lies at the self-actualization or esteem levels rather than lower on the pyramid; that satisfiers are much more likely to appeal to the doubting buyer than hygiene arguments; and that by building positive rewards into these areas, you can develop a force field that can help prospects to satisfy their own buying urges. Let's look at some approaches to accomplishing this.

If prospects have such a strong buying urge, why do they resist at all? There are many reasons. Sometimes what you are selling is not exactly what they had envisioned and they are not quite prepared yet to compromise that dream. Or someone else has made an equally appealing offer and they must now make a difficult choice. Or what you are offering will cause them to make compromises somewhere else in their lives, and they must balance the one against the other. Or, and this is probably the most common reason for resistance, they simply have not yet reached a sufficient level of trust with you to believe that what you are offering is indeed what they want to buy.

In each of these cases, your task is to increase the forces acting on them to move them toward a positive decision in your favor. Remember, they are battling between maintaining the status quo and redefining it. Before you can eliminate resistance, however, you must ventilate it, bring it out into the open where both you and the customer can respond to it. Your first step, therefore, whenever you run across resistance, is to ask questions in order to uncover both the source of the resistance and how strong it is. The questions you ask should uncover one or more of the seven major sources of resistance that create negative force fields moving the prospect away from the desired decision. On the following pages you'll find each of them described along with suggestions you can use to help dissolve the resistance.[5]

Parochial Self-Interest

This simply means "What's in it for me?" The prospect must be shown one or more personal benefits in this instance. In

[5]The discussion of the seven major sources of resistance on this and the following pages is based on the work of Dr. Beverly Hyman and is taken from the American Management Association's course "Training the Trainer."

the case of the sales approach called consultative selling, the benefit is in dollars, the return on investment in the sales representative's proposal. When selling to individuals or families, this resistance is most likely to stem from esteem, safety, or ego needs. In any event, a few open-ended questions should allow the prospect to ventilate the resistance and so bring it out into the open for you to respond to by demonstrating strongly the benefits of purchasing. This will lessen the resistant force field and increase the positive one that both you and the prospect want.

Lack of Trust

Do you remember our discussion in Chapter 6 on the need for trust and the several ways of acquiring it? If you feel that the prospect's resistance comes from a lack of trust, you must find ways to demonstrate that you are a straight shooter who has that prospect's interests in mind. You can do so in several ways. One is by proving that you are a man or woman of your word. Make a promise and then move heaven and earth to fulfill it. If I say I will call at a certain time, I will call at exactly that time. When I set a deadline for delivery, I may be early but I will never be late. Say, "I can have that for you by Friday," and then deliver it on Thursday.

One of my favorite means of gaining trust is by simple self-disclosure. I believe in being very frank and open with customers, so I'll say, "How do I go about doing business with you?" or, "I'd really like to work with you on this. What can I do to get you to buy from me?" Or, if the customer seems remote or vague, I'll say, "I get the impression that you're not comfortable with what I've been saying. Is there a problem?" All of these are statements of honest, open sincerity. They disclose my state of mind or my intentions and, as a result, they build trust by informing the prospect that I am open and honest, that I don't play games.

Finally, by allowing prospects the time and space to think and react to your selling situation, you break the stereotype of a pushy salesman and demonstrate a real concern for their interests. They begin to believe that they can trust someone who is genuinely concerned for their welfare.

Different Assessments and Information About the Purchase

Again, this source of resistance relates to the material covered in Chapter 6. If the prospect's assessment of the value or appropriateness of what you are selling differs from your own, you will never close this person. You must find out what evaluation prospects place on your product or service and how they came by that judgment. When I was selling mutual funds years ago, I had a prospect say, "Oh, I'd never buy your fund. My brother-in-law had a terrible experience with it." So long as she felt that way I couldn't possibly hope to sell her any shares. I had to ventilate that resistance and clarify with her both what her assessment was and what mine was. It turned out that her brother-in-law had indeed had a bad experience, but with a mutual fund that I wasn't selling. Only when the difference is out in the open can you develop an honest, open, trusting relationship. And only then can true win/win selling take place. Incidentally, this prospect eventually bought my fund and became one of my best customers.

Low Tolerance for Change

There are people in the world who no matter how badly they want or need something simply cannot make up their minds to buy it. These folks can waste a great deal of a salesperson's time because they want to go over and over each aspect of the sale and even then are very hesitant to decide. They are also the ones who, at the last moment, sometimes even after the deal is closed, will change their minds. As with anyone who fears anything, after you have ventilated their fears and uncertainties you must build their confidence in themselves, in your product or service, and in you. You may have to take them by the hand and lead them through all of the possible doubts they may have and promise them (truthfully only) the tiniest risk imaginable. The force field that moves them must be strong enough to overcome the safety and security doubts that prevent them from making a decision.

When I suspect that a prospect has a low tolerance for change, I do two things. First, I concentrate on those elements of whatever I am selling that are, or appear to be, similar to what is familiar to the prospect. If I sell computers, I talk about how closely they resemble typewriters. I demonstrate all of the familiar benefits before talking about any of the new ones. I stress how small the change will be. Then I minimize the risk by offering to let my product or service prove itself at no cost. This is where pilot programs or free trial periods can be most effective. They let the low-tolerance-for-change folk get used to the new element with little or no risk. When you succeed, the people suffering from this low tolerance for change are usually so relieved to have made a decision that they will immediately be very grateful to you for helping them to make up their minds.

Fear of Losing Face

No one wants to look bad. This is the expression of a strong ego and esteem need. Unfortunately, it can even stretch down into the safety and security needs range where it is very difficult to overcome. Once your questions have allowed customers to ventilate their doubts, you must build a positive force field to apply pressure in the direction of enhancing reputation and adding to a very fine image at minimal risk to prestige. You must make the decision to buy a positive image builder and the decision not to buy a greater risk. Life insurance has long been sold this way. It works.

Peer Pressure

We are all familiar with the expression, "What will the neighbors think?" I know of executives who are afraid to buy the luxury car they yearn for or the house of their dreams for fear of what their peers may think of them. Or worse, their customers. This can be a very powerful source of resistance. There are really only two ways that I know of to approach the problem. The sounder approach psychologically is to sell the peers first; then those who are heavily influenced by them will easily follow and buy too. Of course this is not always possible, so the other alternative is to discover through questioning how deeply your prospects respect their peers and to redefine the relationship, if possible, so that the person you are selling to can be seen as the trendsetter or leader. Both approaches appeal to your prospects' desire to buy and concurrent need for assurance that they will not be thought badly of by their peers.

Impact of First Impressions

Most of us have the wasteful habit of making snap judgments and then behaving as if they were well thought out. We frequently decide whether or not we like something at the moment of first contact, and then, if that judgment is challenged, devote our intelligence to defending why we were right. How much better it would be to withhold judgment until we have had a chance to better understand what we are seeing and then to decide with care.

Unfortunately, most customers fall into this spur-of-the-moment pattern. It is your job as an effective seller to help them to withhold final judgment until they fully understand what they are buying (or deciding not to buy) and to provide them with the rationale and the justification for buying. You can do this by carefully framing your procedure right up front.

Tell prospects how you want to approach selling them. Set up an agenda or even a schedule. Say that this is a first meeting and that in it you'd like only to explore the prospect's potential. If there is one, you can come back at a later date for a full presentation, then set up a demonstration, and, finally, if the prospect is interested, arrange for a trial period. Set the stage. Explain each step of the process before you take it and then, from time to time, review what you've done so far.

When you do this you are framing the prospects' expectations and then fulfilling them. There is no better way to manage first impressions. Once prospects have made a negative snap decision, however, it is much harder to bring them around to any other view. What this means for selling is that those first few moments are crucial. First impressions are lasting ones and so they must be made to be good ones.

In these last two chapters we've been discussing how to manage those vital first impressions both by creating relationships and by asking questions. But every sale must move beyond the first few minutes. And no matter how skilled a questioner you are, sooner or later you will need to move on to the presentation step in the selling cycle. It is time to turn to that step now.

8

Presenting Solutions to Customer Problems

Effective selling addresses the precise need of the prospect. A presentation that "sells" is one that speaks to the buying need of prospects and provides them with the necessary rationale, desire, and justification for making a decision. Such a presentation must be persuasive, not as a means of influencing or manipulating prospects but, rather, as a means of bringing them to a realization that this product or service is the best available answer to their need or desire to buy. Every day all of us face a number of choices on how to distribute our limited resources in order to attain the most efficient or beneficial return. We want to buy everything but must weigh each potential purchase against others in order to create the greatest benefit for ourselves. It is in this process that the need for persuasion and effective presentation becomes imperative for the would-be effective seller.

So what persuades the customer? More than 2,000 years ago, the Greek philosopher Aristotle said that making an appeal to others that was rational (possessed logos), emotional (possessed pathos), and ethical (possessed ethos) would at least affect them even if it did not totally persuade them. Today Aristotle's insights still hold true. In order to be persuasive you must provide those you wish to persuade with:

- A logical rationale for deciding in your favor
- A positive feeling that what you want for them is good and that you are completely sold on the idea yourself
- An authoritative form of justification that assures them that they are quite right to decide in favor of your product or service—because it will be good for them

Logic, emotion, and justification may not always persuade your customers to buy from you but will always make them think seriously about whether or not to do so. If you apply persuasive pressure by including each of these three persuasive factors in your presentation, if you present to customers at the key moment in their buying cycle, and if you have established the clear need for your customers to purchase a product or service to satisfy their craving to buy, a well-crafted persuasive argument cannot fail. There are several ways to incorporate these three elements into your presentations. Let's examine each one in turn.

Logic

Logic is best shown by outlining some rational structure that leads to the conclusion that buying now is the best possible answer to the problem. This means creating a logical framework or structure for your presentation. It is never what we say but rather how we say it, the order or sequence of it, that most influences how people respond to us. As a salesperson your task is to make your offer rational, logical, and therefore as accessible as possible to the customer, and it is the structure or order of your presentation that makes this possible—or, when it is poorly done, impossible.

The rationale you create puts your message into a comprehensible logical structure. Much of the recent research in the field of neurology, involving the study of the reactions of newborn infants to various gentle stimuli, demonstrates that all knowledge is structure. The doctors are trying to discover how we learn things. What they are observing is that even as early as minutes after birth the human mind is able to distinguish between an image and the background against which that image is discernible. Psychologists have long called this kind of structural relationship a *gestalt,* meaning a pattern of separate phenomena that are seen as distinct figures against a less clearly defined background and yet linked together as one structural impression.

By seeing one thing in contrast to the other things around it, we create a mental, or rational, relationship between them. This is what I mean when I say that all knowledge is structure and that the structure of your presentation gives it its rationale. We compare each new image or piece of information we come across in life with what we already know and, in the light of that comparison, we interpret the new item and give it a meaning in the context of the known. So, when you want to persuade someone to buy your product or service, you must present it in a context that allows this structuring process to happen in your favor. The secret to doing this is to align your efforts to the needs and desires of the customer. Present your product or service in a manner that most closely parallels the way in which that customer thinks.

There are at least five powerful structural patterns that encourage easy access by a listener to the content you want to convey. In order from most powerful to least, they are:

1. Contrast. If the basic working pattern of the human brain is one of contrasting the new with the already known, any approach that contrasts one element with another will have appeal and will be easily understood by your prospect. Contrasting your services with those of your competitor is a strong approach when there are real differences. Contrasting before and after situations has sold many products over the years. Weighing the pros and cons of whether or not to spend the money is a classic "Ben Franklin" close. It works in part because it has such a strong and powerful structure. You can capitalize on this habit of the mind by contrasting colors, sizes, performance levels, features, degrees of comfort, histories, test results, in fact almost anything that is of interest to the prospective customer.

2. Problem/Solution. We love to solve problems. We are

as curious as cats. Show most of us a problem and this special variation of contrasting elements will intrigue us. This is why we play games, follow sports, read thrillers and detective stories. It is why we like crossword puzzles, acrostics, and Trivial Pursuit. And it is why television soap operas and game shows are so popular. The difficulty in using this structure for a sales presentation comes from the equally potent fact that few people like to have their own problems pointed out to them. But if your customer is already aware of the problem and is actively looking for a solution, your job is one of gaining credibility rather than of selling a product or service. The customer only wants a solution and will buy from the first person who provides a credible one. This is why consultative selling is directed at the most universal problem in business, how to make a greater profit. It is also why problem solvers succeed at selling where mere vendors fail.

3. Cause/Effect. Cause and effect constitute another contrast relationship. It is the simple logic of it that appeals. When we present a cause-and-effect relationship, we are saying that one thing or event creates another in logical sequence. Setting your product or service in a relationship that expresses a cause or an effect desired by the customer is a powerful persuader. This particular contrast works very well in situations in which you can set the problem up in a cause-and-effect relationship and then show how, with the addition of your service or product, the cause-and-effect relationship is changed into a solution.

4. Progressive order. The fourth powerful structure is simply any logical arrangement you choose to illustrate your appeal. It can be a sequence of numbers or an alphabetical sequence; a right to left or a clockwise presentation; a morning, afternoon, evening structure; an arrangement of various colors, sizes, shapes, categories; and so forth. The key to its use is simply to carefully underline and signpost the order you have chosen so that the customer can follow it easily. By "signpost" I mean that you must provide clear indications of each number or aspect of the sequence and frequently let the customer know where you are in your progression through that sequence. Such information operates very much like road or street signs. It lets people know where they are.

5. Anecdotes. The fifth and final powerful structure is the telling of a story. Every major religion I know of is illustrated and taught through stories. We love them. Television is little more than a never-ending series of stories of varying lengths, from 15-second commercials to 15-hour miniseries, from sports events to news "stories." It is our love of stories that makes jokes so popular. It is also the source of the very effective (and very old) "third party close" in which the salesperson tells of another customer or relative who also was in doubt about buying but tried the product and found it to be the best decision he or she had ever made.

One of my own favorite formats for exerting persuasive pressure is best expressed by the acronym EASE. It uses a strong problem/solution format. The first two steps are an example of standard inductive logic and are thus a strong structure. They define the problem:

- *E* stands for *Example.* Start your presentation with a single strong, clear, specific example of the problem.
- *A* stands for *Amplify,* so the second step is to amplify on the example, showing how extensive the problem is and how it is related in a cause-and-effect sequence to the detriment of the customer.
- *S* stands for *Specify.* In this step you outline your solution to the problem. Frequently this is a negotiation step in which the customer asks questions and gives information as well as weighs the merits of your solution.
- *E* stands for *Execute #1.* It means that at this point you either unilaterally take the first step or perform an action that is part of the solution you are offering. For example, it can be filling out an order form or, as I frequently do, showing a fully worked-up projection of the results prospects can expect when they sign the order. You are letting prospects know that you have

already begun working for them by taking some action that gets the ball rolling toward your solution to their problem.

Many of the participants in my seminars have initially fought me on this last step. "That's very pushy," they cry, or, "I could never do that to a customer." What is happening is that they imagine it to be the worst kind of hard sell; but my approach to it is not at all hard sell. The problem is this: How many times have you decided after leaving a particular store or vendor that it was offering a pretty good deal after all, and so you went back to buy whatever it was that you'd wanted only to find that the item had been sold to someone else in the interim? I'm sure everyone has missed out at least once or twice because of indecision. I know I have. How often have you been with others, socially or at a business meeting, when everyone agrees that something must be done, some action taken, and yet no one seems to get started? "Execute #1" is designed to prevent these misfires. Remember, only 7½ percent of the population is self-starting. Most people would rather let someone else start the ball rolling. It is much easier than doing so themselves.

It needn't be a heavy-handed push in which you announce "I've already filled in your name and address here on the order form. If you'll just sign your name with this pen I'm slipping into your hand, we can get this order on its way!" It should, instead, be something more on the order of, "I've taken the liberty of running these projected figures into your latest sales forecast and, with your okay today, we could see you back in the black within six months." You've gone ahead unasked and performed a service for the customer. There is a sense that things have already begun to show results. And it sells—not by force (which never persuades) but by recognizing the customer's need and responding appropriately to it.

Emotion

The emotional dimension of your presentation must produce a desire in the customer to want to buy what you are selling. Elements contributing to this emotional dimension include:

- The physical setting in which you show or demonstrate your product (for example, the attractiveness of an automobile or furniture showroom)
- The breadth of your appeal (that is, the number of people who will benefit by the sale)
- The uniqueness of the product or service you offer (for example, that it is the last one, specially customized, or one of a kind)
- Your credibility as an expert in the goods or services you sell—in other words, the confidence and authority you project
- Whether customers can identify with you (through being in the same industry, having the same family status, or being similar in age, sex, educational background, or style of dress)
- Your attitude, including the courtesy and respect you show your customers, your concern for their welfare, your consistency in the claims and promises you make, and your sense of humor
- The amount of enthusiasm and conviction you show

Expressing any or all of these adds to your persuasive impact. How you do so is entirely a matter of individual temperament and style. I can only advise you to take advantage of as many of them as you can if you want to enhance your persuasive appeal. By the same token, incorporating a negative element in any of these can be expected to detract from your presentation and ability to persuade.

Authority

Authority and justification are created by specific details. Statistical, monetary, or numerical proofs are very hard to argue with. Testimonials tend to be strong persuaders as well. After all, with all due respect to Joe DiMaggio and his phenomenal baseball career, does he really know any more than I do about coffee makers? Yet when someone we trust, some figure with whom we can identify, endorses a product or service, we feel persuasive pressure. Professional credentials also inspire instant credibility: We have faith in the airline pilots who fly us and in the doctors who treat us.

To use the persuasive power of authority, you should provide documentation for any claims you make. Offer to perform pilot or trial studies. Cite other respected users of your product or service. Give references before being asked. Use strong nonverbal authority messages. Dress for both credibility and authority. Bring along technical experts, but be sure that they know what their role is and that they leave the talking and questions to you. All of these things can add persuasive authority to your presentations.

People also feel pressure when an appeal is made to their sense of ethics. Public broadcasting stations have capitalized on this aspect of persuasive power for many years. And, lest I be misunderstood, such appeals are not wrong, nor are they necessarily highly manipulative ploys (though they can be misused in that way). They are simply factors that have been observed and studied and that do add persuasive impact to any argument or presentation.

The Sales Presentation

"So what's so special about this laptop computer?" the customer asks.

"Oh, well," the sales representative replies, "it's a 12 Mega Hertz, 286, zero-wait laptop with a built-in 25-millisecond 1:1 interleave hard disk and only 8½ pound portability."

"Oh, I see," says the customer, wondering what on earth a 1:1 interleaf is.

I'm sure you're familiar with such a scene. Time and time again I hear salespeople completely deluge their prospects with such techno-babble. Does it help them to sell? Of course not. Does it impress the customer? Perhaps, but it also locks that customer out of any understanding of the product or service and does much more to hinder the decision to buy than it does to help it. So why do salespeople insist on dumping reams of useless data on prospects?

They do it because they are taught (rightly) to understand what they are selling. They are given sufficient product information to enable them to explain how the product works or what the ramifications of the service they are offering are. The problem is that, unless they are talking to an engineer who speaks the same technical language, the product knowledge they have is too advanced for practical purposes and probably quite a bit over the heads of their prospects. Using such expertise openly merely confuses them. But this "special knowledge" also is a source of credibility. So, when sales representatives feel threatened by an objection or question, or even by the nonverbal behavior of the customer, they may fall back upon product knowledge to regain a sense of control and a feeling of security. And by doing so, they usually turn the customer off.

But, you say, surely salespeople *must* have product knowledge. Yes, they must. No one wants to buy from representatives who know nothing about what they are selling. Unfortunately, most of the sales training done in the United States is intense training in product knowledge *only*. Customers, with the exception of those who are technical experts, and even these people most of the time, are not really interested in the features or even the advantages the product or service has over its competitors. They simply want to know what purchasing the service or product is going to do for them. Period.

Do you really care whether the laptop is a 286 or an 86030? I know the difference, but, because I don't service either of them, I couldn't care less. What would influence my decision to buy one or the other is the effect it would have on my work with the computer. I don't need a name or a number or technological mumbo jumbo to comprehend that benefit. I simply need to know what the benefits of ownership will be.

In other words, features and advantages simply do not sell. Only benefits do. Every salesperson should know exactly which features provide which benefits to the customer and which features provide advantages over the competition, but not every customer needs to know these things in order to make a decision. For example, why do you buy a car with a 3-

liter engine rather than one with only 2.8 liters? Is it the liters or the power and performance? In fact, is it the power and performance, or is it really the extra surge of acceleration that you get with the bigger engine? How often do you plan to disassemble the engine to admire the 3 liters? Probably never. But you'd most likely enjoy that surge of power when you wanted to scoot ahead briskly. And so, you really buy the bigger engine because of the benefit it brings you and not because of its size per se.

The Presentation Matrix

To help you to properly plan benefits into your presentations, I'd like to share with you my Presentation Matrix (Figure 8-1), which shows the sales presentation as measured in two dimensions: product knowledge and degree of responsiveness to the customer. These dimensions are considered from the perspective of the salesperson. The lower left quadrant represents the state of affairs in the sales presentation of the laptop computer mentioned at the beginning of this section; the salesperson has a great deal of product knowledge but very little sensitivity to the customer. Consequently the presentation is filled with jargon, and is essentially boring in its overemphasis on detail. The customer will feel pressured and, if he or she buys at all, will most likely have unrealistic expectations that will lead to fulfillment problems. Unrealistic expectations almost always result from the customer's misunderstanding, which leads to an incorrect interpretation of a technical explanation.

The upper right quadrant shows the opposite situation in which the salesperson is very responsive to the customer but has little or no technical knowledge with which to shape the presentation. These situations lead to unfulfilled promises that tend to buffalo the prospect into buying. There is a loss of credibility when the customer begins to realize that the salesperson doesn't know much about the product or service. And if the customer has been persuaded to buy by the promises of the sales representative, there will almost surely be back-end or fulfillment problems. Except by chance, the prod-

Figure 8-1. Presentation matrix.

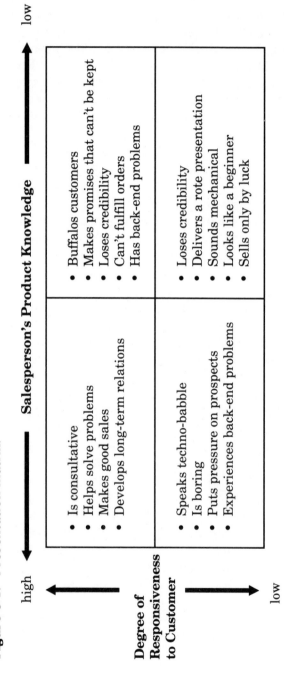

uct or service will probably not be able to deliver all of the promised benefits, and so both the salesperson and the company represented lose their credibility.

In the worst possible case, illustrated in the lower right quadrant, the salesperson is both ignorant of what is being sold and lacks sufficient responsiveness to the customer. The presentation becomes mechanical and sounds like a rote delivery. The customer gets the impression that the salesperson says the same thing to everyone. As a result, the salesperson loses all credibility and frequently looks like a beginner with a memorized spiel. When such approaches succeed they do so usually by luck. The prospect really wanted to buy what was being sold and didn't care how (or even whether) it was presented. We have all experienced this approach when we have been called by a computerized telephone marketing system or a live but inexperienced scripted telemarketer. And this is why both of those sales approaches depend heavily on large numbers of calls with very low response rates. Unless the called party is ready to buy there is seldom a sale.

The ideal situation is illustrated in the upper left quadrant. Here the salesperson is very knowledgeable about what is being sold and yet, at the same time, is governed by a strong sense of concern for the customer's needs and responses. All of the product knowledge is applied to making benefit statements while avoiding techno-babble. As a result, the customer perceives the sales representative as a consultant. The presentation becomes a problem-solving session rather than a high-pressure sales situation. The end result is much more likely to be a closed sale that has few back-end delivery problems and on which a trusting, dependable relationship can be built.

You can use the matrix to evaluate your planned presentation once you have decided what you want to stress. Create benefit statements for every advantage and feature and work out ways to avoid becoming too technical. The matrix will help you to maintain a balance among customer need, responsiveness, and product knowledge as you refine and finally deliver your formal presentation.

Of course not every presentation will make a sale. No

matter how well you have planned it, the customer is almost certain to raise questions or to want to refine the solutions you have suggested. Consequently, most presentations eventually become the basis for negotiating the solution to the customer's problem. The clearer and more persuasive the presentation, the clearer and more likely to succeed will be the negotiation. That's the topic for the next chapter.

9

Negotiating the Terms of the Solution Presented

Most sales literature makes the point that objections are not negative. They are welcome signs of interest. Why do you raise an objection when you are weighing a purchase? My own objections usually stem from one of three areas. First, I object when I don't feel clear in my mind about how strong my desire to buy is. I may need more information (that is, more clearly defined benefits) or merely more enthusiasm or sense of justification than I have been brought to up to this moment.

The second reason that prompts me to raise an objection is that I feel pressured by the salesperson and want to create some breathing room, have a chance to back off from the pressure, take time to think. Like most folks, I don't like to be sold . . . but I love to buy. When I feel I'm being sold, I instinctively back off by raising tough objections.

And my third reason is that sometimes I simply feel too strong a reluctance to change. In Kurt Lewin's terms, there is a stronger force holding me in the status quo than there is moving me to change by making a positive decision to buy. I'm afraid to actively make up my mind and so I make it up passively by doing nothing, by not buying. These appear to be the universal sources of objections, and all of the variations on them can be explained in terms of one or the other.

Smoke Screen vs. Real Objections

Each of these objections of mine is in fact a smoke screen. I certainly don't want to say to the salesperson that I'm hesitant about making a decision so, instead, I say something like, "Well, it looks interesting, but I'd like to run it past my wife (or accountant, or board of directors, or some such) before I make a decision." Although I could say, "Look, you are pressing too hard and I don't like it, so back off," I don't want to hurt the salesperson's feelings or to have a confrontation so I say, instead, "Well, it looks interesting, but I've got to look at a few more competitors and so I'll let you know." Of course I don't want to spend any more for something than I have to, but, in addition, perhaps I don't want to haggle, and I certainly don't want to give away my final price too early in the negotiation, so I say, "It looks nice but it's a bit high on the price scale for me," or some such other price evasion. And I never want to admit, "I'm really pretty slow-witted here so I don't understand what you're telling me." Instead I'll make up some easy fib like, "Yeah, well, I'm not really quite in the market right now. Maybe sometime later, okay?"

If an objection is unspecific, like those just mentioned, chances are that it is really a smoke screen hiding one of the real reasons I've listed. But even salespeople with the skill to recognize such objections for what they are often blow the sale away by responding confrontationally, or by ignoring the objection, or by trying to inundate the poor prospect with product knowledge. Sometimes they actually succeed in rekindling the customer's interest despite their poor handling of the objection and can then say, "But I've saved many a sale that way!" Possibly that's true, but if so it is more by good luck than by good presentation skills.

Of course all objections aren't smoke screens. There are in fact two kinds of objections: smoke screens and real ones, which act as very effective buying signals. A real objection expresses the prospect's interest by raising a concern over whether or not the item or service being sold will in fact satisfy this urge to buy. It tells the salesperson that the prospect really does have a buying urge, that it is active and working at that moment to convince the prospect to buy, and that, within the next few minutes, the prospect will make a decision. All that is needed to close the sale is the help the prospect has asked for. Such an objection is not a smoke screen. It is a buying signal. "So," you ask, "how can I tell the difference?" I know of only one way: Ask the prospect to tell you which it is.

Imagine that you are in a strange city and, having a few hours before you are scheduled to leave, you decide to look for a pair of shoes. You enter a shoe store and ask to see several pairs in your size. The clerk brings the shoes but you see immediately that these shoes are nowhere near the quality you are used to buying. How do you respond? Do you stay a while and try on a few pairs anyway just to make the clerk feel better? Do you immediately complain to the clerk that the store sells poor-quality shoes and that you will never darken its door again? Or do you simply say, "Thank you very much. None of these is quite what I'm looking for. Perhaps some other time," and turn to leave the store?

The clerk must respond in order to save the sale. Let's assume that this is a male clerk and that I am the customer. He can either accept my objection and let me go, which is poor selling technique, or he can ask me to clarify it. In effect, I have raised a smoke-screen objection, and the clerk, in order to sell me a pair of shoes, must discover whether my objection is real or not. He must find out why I raised the objection. As I've just pointed out, the simplest way of doing so is to ask me directly. He might say something like, "Of course. What is it that you were looking for? We have many other lines and perhaps one of them would be more to your taste?" Now I must either make up another smoke-screen objection, firmly reject doing business of any kind with this shop (a full rejection, not an objection), or tell the clerk that I don't like the quality of the shoes he brought out (the real objection).

We will look in a moment at what to do if I provide another smoke-screen objection. But if I respond by telling the truth, the clerk has a chance to show me a pair of shoes that might appeal to my urge to buy. If the store has a pair I'll probably buy them and both the clerk and I will be happy.

If the store doesn't have a pair, there will be no sale. If the clerk tries to sell me shoes that are inferior, or not what I am looking for, there will still be no sale, but I will now feel resentment and begin to resist the clerk's sales efforts strongly. After all, I can't be sold what I don't want except perhaps by deception or coercion.

On the other hand, even if the other lines are still not quite up to my standards but I think one or two pairs might be acceptable, I'll probably try them on. If I like them but they are not quite perfect, I'll say something like, "These are not quite right. The left one pinches a bit and I don't like the color. Can you get me a half size larger on the left foot in a darker shade?" This is a real objection. No matter how impossible it may be to satisfy my demand, I have indicated clearly that I am interested and am even enjoying the product but that it isn't quite right yet. Your task, if you were the clerk, would be to respond positively to my objection and begin to negotiate with me to satisfy my urge. By expressing the objection, I have indicated a strong urge to buy. It is the best buying signal there is. It says that I am seriously considering a purchase, that I want to make it now, and that I merely need a little help from the salesperson to resolve the doubt or reservation in my mind.

Responding to Objections

Real objections are pure gold to the skilled salesperson. Even when they appear to be negative they are clear-cut and serve as the reality on which any successful negotiation must be based. The prospect may indeed be following a game plan of checking out three or four people and you are the first one on the list. Or, perhaps the price really is much higher than the prospect anticipated and so becomes a real issue. I know many people who would not dare to make an important decision without consulting their boss, or their spouse in a consumer sales situation, and still others who might dare but who want their boss or spouse to be part of such a decision. As a salesperson, should you interfere with their practices? If you try, you will alienate them and lose the sale. Real objections are open invitations to help in satisfying the buying urge. Help those who raise them on their own terms and you will sell.

So what should you say, how should you respond to smoke screens? The first and most important step in responding to any objection is to ventilate the cause of the objection. By "ventilate," I mean that your task is to help prospects to articulate the real reason for hesitation, to express the real objection. It may be exactly what they are saying it is. But it may be a smoke screen like the ones I've mentioned earlier. If you guess, you may be wrong and will surely lose some sales. If you assume you know the cause, you will also surely be wrong a good percentage of the time. The only way to be certain is to ask. Ask honestly. The prospects who want or need to buy will gladly let you know the source of their anxiety if you help them to express it. If the objection is real, answer it and close. If the objection is a smoke screen, you must get the real one out or there will be no sale.

Begin by responding to the objection with a question that sidesteps the obvious point of the objection and invites the customer to explain why it was raised. One of the oldest and best formats for doing this is to say, "You must have a reason for saying that. May I ask what it is?" This phrase, or whatever variation of it you feel comfortable with, works because it is not a manipulative tool but rather a polite invitation to the prospect to explain his or her objection. It is, in effect, permission to be honest, and as such it is a difficult invitation to refuse. In my experience, no one who really has a buying need will refuse it. Those who refuse it either do not really have a need that can be satisfied or they are so afraid of being manipulated that they will refuse to make any purchase until that fear is dealt with.

Most of the time asking for the prospect's reason will air the true objection. Even when it elicits only another smoke-screen objection, you should proceed in the same manner. Ask the customer for a commitment at this point. You are saying in effect that you are serious and will work hard from this point onward to satisfy prospects' concerns and buying needs.

But, in return, you need to feel that they are serious, too, and so you ask for a commitment. The tried and true formula for doing so is to ask, "If I can solve that problem, will you buy my product (or service)?" Once again, there is no need to use these exact words. You will, in fact, be more effective if you can translate the expression into words that match the situation and speak the customer's language.

"If I can solve that problem, will you buy my product?" is a direct, unequivocal close. It fulfills the role requirement of being a salesperson and the expectation of the potential customer of being asked to buy something. My customers usually smile and agree or tell me their real objections in response to it. In any event, you will get either a yes or a no answer at this point. If it is yes, negotiate a solution to the problem and close. If it is no, ask why again. This time you might express your puzzlement or confusion and ask for clarification. Remember, you are helping the customer to ease his or her own discomfort by creating positive forces to move the decision toward the sale. Indecision is uncomfortable for the prospect. A decision against you is uncomfortable for you. The only real win/win game possible at this stage is for you to resolve the customer's doubt by helping him or her to decide.

Furthermore, it would be pointless for you to proceed to work on the problem with no commitment on the part of the prospect to reward you for your effort. That simply wouldn't be fair. Yet I have run into customers, as I'm sure you have, who will try such tactics, and salespeople who will foolishly spin their wheels in response. People who use this tactic are afraid that they will be taken advantage of. They are afraid that they won't get the best deal possible. They are playing a win/lose game because they simply do not yet trust you. It is here that you must win their trust if you don't already have it. Remember, none of us likes to buy from someone we can't trust. But even the most demanding and difficult customers will buy from you if they come to trust you. So disclose. Express your genuine concern and ask them to explain themselves.

As you know from your reading of chapters 5 and 6, trust

comes in large part through self-disclosure. So now is the time to openly share your feelings with your prospects. Usually I only have to confess my disappointment or confusion at their responses to elicit the truth. I'll say, "Let me be open with you and share with you how puzzled I am," or "When I came here today I really hoped to be able to reach some level of agreement with you. I'm very frustrated and puzzled, frankly, about how to proceed from here. What can we do to make this a productive meeting for both of us?"

Once, I was sitting across the desk from a man who was obviously lying to me. I could see it, but what could I do? There was no way to say "You are a liar" and still make a sale. The only phrase that came to mind was one I had heard years before in a training film and that I had laughed at uproariously for how silly and artificial it sounded. But I could think of nothing else, so I said, "I hear you saying _____ , but let me share with you what my reaction is to what you've just been saying. It doesn't sound true to me. I don't feel that you're being as open with me as I am with you." He looked at me for a moment and then smiled and began to laugh. "As a matter of fact, I'm not," he said. "Here's what the problem is," and he proceeded to be very open and honest with me. I have used that phrase maybe a dozen times in my selling career and it has worked every time. It is the only way I know of telling people that they are lying without insulting them. And it helps them to keep their dealings with you straight as well.

The Negotiation Stage of Selling

In sum, then, a real objection is a strong buying signal. Drawing out an objection is one of the goals of a good presentation because it tells the salesperson that the customer is near the decision point. So one of your purposes in a sales presentation is to draw out the real objection. As I've explained, the best way to do this is to return the objection in the form of a question that asks the prospect to clarify, explain, or justify that objection. If it is real, it will become immediately apparent. If it is not, accept whatever rationale the prospect gives and respond with a conditional close: If you can solve their problem, will they buy? This procedure places you in the negotiation stage of the sale.

All things are negotiable. Sooner or later even fixed prices must change, so with enough power (or pull or authority) fixed rules and prices can be made to bend. Timing the negotiation is the crucial step. Because this is so, everyone buying from you wants to feel that they are dealing at exactly the right time to get the best possible deal and that they are dealing with the right authority who has the power to bend the rules a bit in their favor. These two elements, time and power, coupled with a third, information, are the potent variables that make or break negotiations. Often, in fact, formal negotiations become merely struggles over which side controls one or more of these elements.

The most skilled salesman I ever worked with used to pride himself on closing customers in such a way that they never knew they had been closed. His skill was in marshaling the three negotiating elements so that all of the psychological forces to buy were enhanced and aided by them. Having asked and discovered early in the sales cycle the degree of strength of the buying need, he would build on it during his presentation, removing obstacles and countering pressures to hesitate or deny. He would help the prospect to create a strong positive sense of desire. He wouldn't even try to close until he was sure of the pressure level of desire that had built up. He was never in a hurry to close, letting the time pressure build on the prospect, not on himself. He would simply keep sounding prospects out for how they felt and how they were responding to his service. Once he was sure of having all of the motivational information available, he would review it with the prospect and then ask for the order. He got it more times than anyone else I've worked with.

Both time and information are key sources of power or leverage in selling. The purpose of proper planning, of qualifying customers for their buying cycles, is related to the need for the effective seller to call only at the appropriate time. If you know when the customer needs to buy and what time constraints he or she is operating under, you will find the sale really quite easy to make. It is when we try to sell prospects outside of the constraints that normally influence their buying urges that we either fail or become pushy and ineffective.

One of the classical bits of selling lore is that persistence wins. Hanging in there eventually makes the sale. It is true. It often does. But it does so because by being patient and not giving up too soon or by not accepting "no" too readily, a salesperson over time builds credibility with the customer. You become someone who can be trusted merely by virtue of being there, by becoming a member of the normal cast of characters with whom the prospect deals.

In addition, as we've seen, most folks buy because they feel a need. This urgency creates time pressure, pressure to decide, now. Good selling, good negotiating means tapping the urgency that customers already feel and using it to help them to satisfy the urge. Thus a part of your negotiation strategy is to trace for customers what will happen if they do nothing, that is, if they fail to make a decision to buy from you. Or you might want to stress the benefits to be derived from their immediate use of their new purchase. This impatience is a common motivator. Think of anything you have bought and then had to wait for shipment on. Isn't it frustrating? This is why most cars are sold off the lot and not ordered on a custom basis from the factory. It is why, although mail-order sales are burgeoning, most merchandise is still sold live in stores and why the great mail-order houses nearly always also have real stores that people can come to and shop in. We want immediate gratification. The effective salesperson closes sales by helping us to attain it.

Of course knowing the buying cycle is a form of information that gives you leverage in any negotiation. If the element of time can be addressed in the planning stage of the sale, information is addressed mainly in the questioning part of the sales call. It is also the essence of Mack Hanan's "consultative selling™,"[1] in which salespersons must immerse themselves in the customer's business, see it from their point of

---

[1] Mack Hanan, *Consultative Selling*, 3rd ed. (New York: AMACOM, 1985).

view, and create solutions for problems that the customer may not yet even be aware of.

Product knowledge, too, naturally fits into the information category. Salespeople who know both their own business and that of their customers will succeed and will become excellent negotiators in the objections and closing parts of the sale. This is so because we are all appreciative of people who know and understand us, who know what we need and when, and who can provide timely service. We also want to be able to depend on those from whom we buy to be there when we need them, to be able to answer our questions and allay our doubts, and to go to bat for us with their own company if we have a problem. The salesperson who does not intimately know his or her own product or service will leave the prospect feeling unsure and tentative about the purchase. As we know from Chapter 8, no one wants to be inundated by a flood of techno-babble, but at the same time no one wants to be told by a salesperson, "I don't know." If at any time you must say that to a customer, add, "But I will have the information for you by _____," and keep your word. This takes care of not having information at your fingertips; it adds to the pressure of time on the prospect, and it builds trust by demonstrating your concern for the relationship.

Time and information give one power or leverage in a negotiation situation. Despite the slightly negative connotations of both of those words, there is no intent to manipulate here. As you know from having read this far, I am strongly opposed to manipulation in sales. It has no place. There are no tricks here, no surefire closes or ways to pull the wool over the customer's eyes. By power or leverage, I mean simply the professional understanding (information again) of the unseen forces at play while prospects make up their minds and of those forces that shape the dynamics between buyer and seller. Knowing and responding to such dynamics allows the salesperson to guide the relationship so as to satisfy the customer's buying need. Any abuse of such understanding leads eventually to the disappointment of the customer and the frustration of the salesperson's efforts to sell.

Honest, nonmanipulative power comes from three

sources. First, it can be felt in the time framing of the relationship and the information base that informs both parties. The one best in control of time and with the most vital data has more power or leverage in any negotiation.

The second source of power or leverage is technique, and here I mean the habit of responding with questions rather than with defensiveness, of thinking and acting in terms of win/win solutions (an ethical appeal) and of behaving openly, honestly, and directly rather than deviously playing games or falling back on memorized product knowledge, catch phrases, or "standardized sales techniques." If the prospect says, "I tried your services and they didn't work for me," don't respond by saying "But we have hundreds of satisfied customers. Our service is the best in the field. The competition has nothing to match us." Instead say, "That's interesting. You obviously have had some experience with our service. What happened?" Such an assertive yet honest technique is an important source of power for those who use it. It is manifest in strong, assertive, confident nonverbal behavior. It shows when the salesperson has a clear-cut objective for the call and pursues it through questions and direct communication.

Finally, power or authority or leverage comes from how we respond to the environment and the available artifacts that show that response. Talking from a raised dais, meeting in a formal office and sitting behind a large desk, sitting at the head of a table whenever possible, dressing the part of an executive, exhibiting polished manners—all denote authority and give one a degree of appropriate leverage or power. Forms of legitimacy such as precedent (it's always done this way), company policy, titles (such as vice president, regional sales manager), and formally written documents (such as standard contracts, mortgages, spec sheets, and so forth) all add authority.

Negotiating Classic Objections

The four classic objections that prospects raise in one form or another are: "I'm not interested," "Not right now, thanks,"

"It's not right," and "It's too expensive." Each of these can be
handled by using one or more of the three negotiating variables we've covered: time, information, or leverage.

"Not interested" should never happen if the salesperson
has done the necessary research and selected the prospect at
a likely interest point. Information and the power to ask
questions are the keys. The classic response "If I can show
you a way to . . . would you be interested?" has a legitimate
purpose here. It seeks more information, asks for a commitment, and directs the interview toward the salesperson's objective.

The best approaches in response to "not interested" are
to review the available information by, say, outlining the costs
to the prospect of no action if you have that person's trust at
this point, or to gather more information, particularly with
regard to buying time frames. "Of course not," you say, "but
can you foresee a time when xyz might occur? I'd like to
present you briefly with the option of my product/service in
the event such a need should arise so that you will have
someone to turn to when it does." And you proceed to ask
questions to find out more and to lock in on the buying cycle.

"Not now" is clearly almost the same situation in that
the prospect is telling you that there is a possibility that he
or she might buy, but in the future. Your response must be to
tie that future down to some form of buying cycle that you
can approach with some hope of a warmer reception. This
should be the response to rejections of any kind. "No" is an
acceptable answer provided you leave the door open for business at a more opportune moment. So this objection too is a
matter of framing time and either gathering or using information.

"It's not right" needs a questioning response. Say something like, "I can see where your applications would certainly
be unique, but perhaps you could help me clarify for myself
the way in which it [my product] is not right." Too often the
salesperson responds to this objection by sounding off with a
tirade of defensive nonsense. What is needed is a question
that will cause prospects to explain and define what they
don't like. Only in this way can the seller solve the problem

and negate the objection. The response is a matter of gathering information and using it to gain the prospect's commitment to a sale by saying "If I can solve that, will you buy?"

Finally, there is the objection tied to price. This one is perhaps the biggest and most feared of all objections, so I've saved it for last. It comes up in all of my seminars, including my courses on formal negotiations. Even when it cannot possibly be an issue, in situations where the price of a commodity is set by a futures market many miles away, people still get hung up on price. They do so because they are knowledgeable about the marketplace and know that there are usually several prices for something, some higher and some lower. They want to be sure they are getting the lower one. They do so because, until they get to know and trust those from whom they buy, they don't trust salespeople to give them the best service at the fairest price. But then all of us are suspicious. And we are so because each of us grows up wanting to feel strong and independent—which means being competent and capable, among other things, of avoiding being cheated. So our self-esteem and ego needs play a major role in the price objection. But if you as the salesperson know what prompts the objection, it is not so very difficult to frame an appropriate response to it.

First of all, you can enhance the customer's sense of security by providing a time frame. Some salespeople offer thirty-day free trials, and American Express offers a full year's "no questions asked" warranty on everything purchased with its card. The effect of these is to create trust. Customers can then say to themselves: "If I don't like it or it doesn't work, I can always take it back. The decision isn't final and if we've been had we'll find out and get our money back. How can we go wrong?" Notice that in this answer price is no longer the issue. Instead it is whether or not the money is well spent, whether or not the customer has been taken advantage of or has the upper hand (admittedly it is a win/lose attitude, but that doesn't make it any the less common).

A different tack, based on using information instead of time, has much the same effect. You can remove the issue of price, as our real estate saleswoman did in Chapter 5, by linking the price to elements the customer has indicated are prime needs. Thus when the client says "$10,000 is just too much," the salesperson's answer is, "Of course. That's no problem. Here is the list of things you have asked us to provide. Which of them can we cut out in order to lower the price for you?" Now every time price comes up, it is a matter of reduced benefit. There is no price disagreement, only a negotiation for benefits. I find this an excellent approach when I believe customers' objections to be tied to the desire to save face, to appear both to their peers and to themselves as competent, skilled negotiators who have not been taken advantage of.

The point of both of these responses is to redefine the issue, to remove it from the customer's definition of price, which is frequently a knee jerk reaction, by placing it squarely in the realm of the customer's real needs or desire for benefits. By using such an approach the salesperson helps the customer to decide. In effect, the salesperson gives the customer permission to buy.

10

Closing From the First Moment of Contact

Many of my clients are concerned because they want their salespeople to "close harder" or "more aggressively." It would seem to be the most logical thing in the world that a salesperson should ask the customer to buy something. Yet it happens far less often than logic says it should. It happens far less often than the many managers who have asked me to train their salespeople to close better would like it to happen. It should be a natural thing to do, and yet it isn't.

All of us did it as children. No one under the age of 14 (and this probably applies to the rest of us over that age too) would hesitate a half second to ask a parent or a sibling for whatever it was that he or she wanted. We are all closers when we aren't thinking about it, when we don't look upon what we are doing as "closing" but rather as asking for something we "need" to have. The problem seems to lie in whether or not we are aware that we are closing. Awareness creates a self-consciousness that makes the act of closing more difficult than it need be.

Getting Rid of the Close

One of my clients simply eliminates the word "close" from his vocabulary in order to get around it. As he points out, "Asking the customer for an order is not an ending, something you 'close off.' It is a beginning. It is the beginning of a relationship. Salespeople should be trained to stop thinking of it as a 'close' and to begin thinking of it as an 'opening,' a beginning!" Absolutely true, but traditionally, for most of the rest of us, it's still a close no matter what it is called.

I think the answer lies in concentrating on the word "close" and realizing its distinct meaning. It isn't the act of closing that has meaning; it's the place of that act in the cycle of selling. Human beings are nearly universally uncomfortable with a lack of closure. For instance, if this sentence . . .

How do you feel? Did you do a double take? Did you loop back to the end of the last paragraph to see if you could pick up the thread or find the pattern? Unconsciously we like whatever has begun to fulfill itself by completing the pattern of its process. In other words, we like endings. We don't like things that start and then fail to finish. We have an inborn sense of closure. We love mystery and suspense stories because they are mysterious or suspenseful and because, at the same time, we know that they will end with the solution given to us and with all the loose ends neatly tied up.

Your prospects are no different. They too want things to play themselves out to their appropriate end. And the proper end of an initiated sales call is to ask for something. In fact, by *not* asking you leave the prospect feeling vaguely uncomfortable about the call. Few will be able to pinpoint why they feel this way, but it will feel incomplete to them and so they will associate you with something vaguely unpleasant. This is not a good role for a salesperson to be cast in.

The most important tool in handling the need to close is setting clear call objectives. You will remember that in Chapter 4 I defined a sales call objective as a description of what the prospect or customer will do, what action he or she will perform, because you made the call. If you have set such a clear action-oriented objective, you know exactly what you will ask your prospect for and it becomes only a matter of finding the right moment to ask. When you combine these two aspects of closing, you will find it much easier to complete the cycle for yourself and for the customer by asking for whatever your objective specified before you made the call.

Closing actually becomes a constructive part of the relationship between the buyer and the seller when you perceive it as a key step toward satisfying the buyer's need and desire to buy. Frequently the reluctance of salespeople to close stems from a sense that in doing so they are somehow intruding on or pushing the customer. Indeed, using mechanical, memorized, scripted closes does do this. But a close that sums up a proper presentation and that arises out of the customer's need to buy becomes a further service that you perform for that customer. It is an authoritative statement that moves the customer toward a decision.

Experienced salespeople are familiar with the elation and gratitude that customers often feel when the salesperson is able to take them off the hook by getting them to make a decision. Once they have made it, the pressure of indecision disappears, the battle between opposing forces is resolved. The decision is made! No more struggle and fret! They are overjoyed. You may feel that I'm exaggerating, but let me ask you, don't you feel relief when a difficult decision is finally made? No one wants to be turned down, but isn't it a relief to finally hear even a "no" from a customer who has been shilly-shallying back and forth for a long time? I have always preferred a "no" to a "maybe." As a result, I get mostly "yeses" because I know that when I ask for the order I am helping that customer to buy, to make a positive decision that will take him off the hook. In fact, shilly-shallying is usually caused by the lack of a firm close. So I ask strongly with no fear of hearing "no." It's no problem.

Bringing the customer to closure carries with it another benefit to the salesperson. It helps to build a relationship of trust between you and your customer. Because there is emotional release with most decisions, you become associated with that release, with that positive feeling. Your customer has invested in you by listening and following your advice and making the decision. Once customers have invested in you, they want to trust you. They want to be reassured that they were right in their decision and so they want to believe in you. This is the essence of trust. It is yours for the asking, but *you must ask*.

Assertiveness vs. Aggressiveness in Closing

In my sales seminars I ask for a show of hands of all those who like to be aggressed against. No hands shoot up. A few people laugh nervously, wondering what I'm getting at. Then I ask them to look in any newspaper help wanted ads under "sales help." I say, "What will most of the ads say?"

"Wanted, aggressive self-starter!" they chorus back.

How did aggression creep into our sales metaphor? Selling shouldn't be aggressive. When someone comes on to me aggressively, I become defensive. Don't you? Even if I want to buy, I know I don't want to buy from someone who is aggressing against me. How can I trust such a person? But I must trust the one I buy from. Those who place the "aggressive" ads say to me, "But you've got it all wrong. Nobody's aggressing *against* the customer." But how can anyone aggress *for?* Aggression means "acting against." It cannot exist without a target. Aggressive closing turns people off and makes them defensive. In fact, a good deal of the sales resistance you encounter in the field is probably caused by salespeople who have tried aggressively to sell something to those poor hapless prospects.

If you're like most folks, right now you are trying to think of ways in which salespeople must be aggressive. After all, you've heard all your life that salespeople have to be aggressive. Even if you've never sold before, you've seen those ads. Deep down, you know a salesperson needs to be aggressive. And you are right! Sales people do need to be aggressive. They must respond aggressively to their competitors or they will be squeezed out of the business. They must respond aggressively to their own habits if they begin to slack off. They must become aggressive gatherers of market information. In all of these tasks the professional salesperson must be aggressive. But no salesperson should try to sell aggressively. It has been my experience that those who are most successful are so because they are *assertive* rather than aggressive. The two are not the same thing at all.

Imagine that you are waiting in a line. Perhaps it is to buy tickets for a movie or a sporting event, or at the checkout counter of your local supermarket. As you stand there, someone casually sidles past you and slips into line ahead of you. What do you do? Stop reading for a moment and think of your answer. Be as honest as you can be.

Your response will fit into one of the following four possible categories: You could be aggressive; you could be passive; you might be passive-aggressive; or you might respond assertively. Let's examine the differences by looking at each one:

• *Aggressive:* You might say something like, "Hey! Who do you think you are? You can't cut in front of me! There's a line here, buddy (or lady). Go to the back of it where you belong." You might even respond (I hope you don't) by grabbing the person and boosting him to the back of the line. You could push him aside. You could even beat him severely about the shoulders while screaming "Line jumper! Line jumper!" at the top of your lungs. All of these actions would be classed as aggressive. And all of them would elicit the same response from the person you do them to: return aggression. When you attack someone or even approach that person aggressively (as unfortunately sometimes happens in sales situations), you provoke him or her to respond aggressively. You create an unmistakable win/lose situation and now you must win it or else. It is this approach that creates the "pushy" stereotypes hung on salespeople in general.

• *Passive:* In a passive response, as the name suggests, you do nothing. Not wanting to be involved in a confrontation, which you know will be the price of an aggressive response, you say nothing and let the line crasher get away with it. Usually you will rationalize the situation to justify your doing nothing about it by thinking something like, "Well, they only have a couple of items. It'll only take a minute longer if they go first. Besides, I'm a kind and generous person so I'll show my magnanimity and let them go ahead of me." You make yourself feel better by salving your ego.

You lie to yourself so that you won't have to accept yourself as less than the strong capable adult you'd like to be. You rationalize away your inaction. This avoids a confrontation, but it also prevents you from meeting your objective in the situation. Furthermore, while you can rationalize to your own ego, others will read that they can get away with cutting in front of you and then will do so. If you wear a sign around your neck that says "doormat," the world will wipe its feet on you. Passive responses lose both win/win and win/lose games. And in sales, accepting "no" too easily leads to an ever-increasing series of rejections.

• *Passive-aggressive:* By far the most common response is this one. A passive-aggressive response is one in which you appear to be passive, in order to avoid the confrontation, while you are plotting secretly to take your revenge! The saying "I don't get mad, I get even!" is the perfect expression of this type of skulking response. In the line, you might slip across the street to get a hot cup of coffee and then accidentally spill it down the line crasher's back. Or you could "inadvertently" run your grocery cart into the back of the crasher's heels.

A salesman once bragged to me that he'd found the perfect response to customers or prospects who were rude enough to hang up on him. He said, "I immediately call them right back and when they answer the phone, I say, 'I owe you one!' and slam down the receiver on them!" I'm sure he feels a lot better when he does this. But I guarantee you he never made a sale that way! Passive-aggressive behavior is pathetic because it never solves a problem and almost always makes situations worse. Vendettas, feuds, and even wars fit into this petty category.

• *Assertive:* In this option you deal with the situation directly, openly, and honestly. You point out to the crashers that they have moved in front of you and that you are made tense and uncomfortable by their behavior. Ask them to move back behind you and express your genuine desire that all of you get checked out quickly or acquire good seats. Some of my trainees have said, "But that's so cumbersome and awkward-sounding. I'd never say that." That's exactly my point.

Most people never behave this way. And yet those few who do end up getting things done their way, or at least to their satisfaction, far more often than those who don't.

Assertive responses work because they are honest, not devious. They work because they address the problem directly without being overbearing or confrontational. They express emotion in a rational way that justifies action. Being assertive addresses the situation directly and rationally and so fosters the likelihood of an acceptable solution.

Assertiveness is a must in selling. Aggressive behavior on the part of a salesperson toward a customer only creates resistance and causes lost sales. Passive salespeople invariably accept smoke-screen objections or neglect to close and so leave both the customer and themselves unsatisfied. I've seen countless salespeople end a presentation and then wait futilely for the customer to close himself. Passive-aggressive behavior can have no role in selling. If you went around trying to get even with all of the people who've said "no" to you, you'd have no time for selling. Actor Danny DeVito has made a wonderful career out of being hilariously passive-aggressive, but he's selling the hilarity, not the passive-aggressiveness.

The whole approach to selling that we've been examining in this book is assertive. If you have a store and advertise, the customer who shows up in response is the one initiating the contact, not the salesperson. But when you must find the right customers, call them, make an appointment to see them, and then interact with them, question them, and help them to come to a decision, you are behaving from the first moment of the sales cycle in an assertive manner.

You have a solution to the customer's need. But the customer will never know that unless you initiate contact and explain how what you sell can satisfy that need. Even knowing that you can do so, the customer may never actually decide to use what you are selling unless you assert yourself and ask for that decision. If there is doubt or indecision remaining, again you must assert yourself to help the customer resolve the dilemma and make the decision, or you will have failed to sell and the customer will be left with an unsatisfied urge to buy that will end up being exercised on a competitive product or service.

Assertiveness is the key. To initiate conversation with a stranger you must be assertive. To address someone else's problems you must be assertive. To help someone to make a decision you must be assertive. Good selling is the art of becoming successfully assertive. But please notice that at no time is this behavior aggressive, manipulative, or abusive of the customer in any way. You have an obligation to help your customers, but you do not have a mandate to force, abuse, manipulate, intrude on, or in any other way offend them.

One of my favorite clients used to say, "I'm happy to accept 'no' from an *informed* prospect." He saw that his obligation was to inform and to offer help. Once he was sure that the customer understood what was being offered and yet still rejected it, he would happily withdraw to find someone else who did want it. "No" *is* an acceptable answer from customers or prospects once they have been informed and offered your services. But because you have an obligation to be sure, the informing and offering cannot be passive. The customers have no reason to believe in or accept passive behavior, and so will not. By the same token, they will not accept aggressive behavior either. No one wants to fight with a customer. Assertive selling is the only possible approach.

Four Rules of Assertive Selling

Aside from deciding to be more assertive, what can you do to become a stronger assertive seller? There are four rules. Follow them and you will become a stronger closer and a more effective sales representative.

First, *have a clear-cut sales call objective.* If you cannot state simply what action you want the customer to take during the call, *don't make the call!* Don't even pick up the telephone unless you know exactly what it is that you want from the customer on the other end of the line. When I train salespeople and go out on calls with them, I ask them to write the objective out in full before the call. I tell them just before going in to glance at it again to be sure that they have it fixed uppermost in their minds.

Ask yourself, "If I'm not going in for a specific purpose, why am I here?" If you allow yourself to get sidetracked, pulled away from that objective, how will you ever achieve it? Everything you do during the call should be directed toward reaching that objective. I call this "closing from the first moment of contact." It works, but only if you have that clear action-oriented objective fixed in your mind.

Second, *let nothing go by.* By that I mean, when the customer makes an unclear remark, or raises an objection, or even rejects your offer, *do not accept it!* Instead, question it. The single most common complaint I get from sales managers all across the country is that their people passively accept anything the customer says. They don't ask for clarification. They don't express doubt. They don't counter. They just passively sit there and accept smoke screens and rejections without even checking to see if the prospect is sufficiently informed or merely expressing concern.

Remember, you are helping people to make a decision. You have the obligation to be sure that they understand the help you are offering. You also have the obligation to be sure that what you are offering is on-line and the right solution for them. You cannot meet either of these obligations by letting objections or evasions go. You must be assertive and ask for clarification. When you do so, you show your customers that you are serious, concerned, and determined. If they are hiding behind manipulative games, you notify them that you are not. You gain credibility and authority and, consequently, control over the sales call.

Third, *don't leave until you get at least one of the things you came for.* This is why it is important to have at least one fallback objective. You will recall that when I discussed framing call objectives I recommended writing down not only the principal thing you wanted to achieve but also what you'd settle for if you couldn't get number one. Having that backup objective allows you to leave and yet remain productive, to prosper with the call even though you must accept less than what you really wanted. It allows you to move the sale forward without becoming aggressive.

You have spent time and effort on the call. To come away empty-handed is a waste of both. It is also a waste of the customer's time and energy. So, *do not* leave until you have made the call productive in some way. If the prospect begins looking at her watch or says, "I've really got to go. I've got another meeting right now," answer by saying, "Of course," or, "I can see you're short of time," and *close.* Ask either for your main objective, if it's appropriate, or for one of your secondary ones. But ask! Say, "So what's the next step. Can I get your commitment to _____ ?" Your prospect has brought up the time issue. Let it work for you, not against you. If your prospect is in a hurry, then she must give you an answer quickly.

"No" doesn't signal the end of the interview. Every TV fan knows actor Peter Falk's famous detective Columbo who ends the interview to put the suspect off guard and then, just as he's leaving, stops, turns, and says, "Oh, I nearly forgot. There is one other thing you could help me with," and continues the interview. It works in sales, too. Some of my best closes have been made while walking to the exit with the customer.

One of the oldest and most effective closes in the consumer selling field is the "closed case" close in which the salesperson, when the customer says "no," agrees and closes his briefcase as a sign that the interview is over. However, the salesperson doesn't get up to leave but rather continues to sit and chat. Sooner or later the subject always returns to the salesperson's product or service and the case gets opened again for further clarification or presentation. The salesperson assertively stays to get what he came for. Can such a technique be abused? Of course it can be, and has been. But if you are selling within the parameters I've laid out in this book, it won't be. Instead, it will merely give your prospects time to get used to the idea of the purchase, to feel less defensive, and to come to grips with their real objections or buying desires. It will help them to make a decision and at the same time fulfill your sales objective.

When the customer says "no" or ends the interview, remember to ask why. People make time for what is most important to them. By not leaving without some form of commitment, you are making yourself someone important enough to make time for. Persistence shows authority and confidence and gains you credibility. Acquiescence shows passivity and lack of conviction and sows seeds of doubt. Hang in there till you get at least some of what you came for.

Fourth, *test yourself*. Put pressure on yourself. As you leave each call, ask yourself, "What changed in there as a result of this call?" If the answer is "nothing," then you've failed. I know of no more effective way to sharpen my own sales performance than by asking this simple question. Either I achieved something or I did not. There are no two ways about it. Either I made my objective or I did not, and if I did not, I have to ask myself, "Why not?" There is no more effective evaluation tool than self-evaluation. Try it. You'll find it improves performance immensely.

These four rules of assertive selling make salespeople strong and confident, and they get results. At the same time, they do not offend customers or aggress against them, nor do they take advantage of them. They merely help salespeople to help their customers through difficult buying decisions.

The Three Most Polished Professional Selling Skills

From time to time someone will ask me to summarize something I've written. They will ask, "What's the essence? If you had to distill the book down to its most important elements, what would they be?" For this book, they would be three essential skills. Practice these and you will be a salesperson *extraordinaire*. I call these the three most polished professional selling skills. Those who practice them effectively are the best professionals in any field. Those who don't, aren't.

Skill number one is *the ability to ask questions*. Salespeople love to talk. But talking never closed a sale. Questions, on the other hand, are the professional seller's best means of gathering information, the most effective means of controlling the sales interview and presentation, the most potent answer to any objection because they make the prospect think, and the single most honest and open closing tool ever devised. Furthermore, because questions require answers, they are the one selling tool that involves customers, sounds out their feelings and needs, pays attention to them, and is solicitous of their welfare. There is no more potent selling skill than the ability to ask questions.

The second greatest skill is closely tied to the first one. It is *the ability to listen.* When I travel and consult around the country, I hear salespeople on the phone or across the desk talking and talking. Talking doesn't sell, listening does. Have you ever found yourself face to face with a salesperson and had trouble interrupting the spiel in order to speak? I have— most of the time when I set out to buy something, in fact. I don't buy from people who won't listen to me, and I don't expect folks to buy from me unless I listen to them. Listening, attending to someone, is the most important degree of responsiveness we can exhibit. And buyer-oriented selling is almost totally responsive.

Listening to what is said both aloud and nonverbally is the surest way for professional sellers to monitor their own progress and the progress of their customers toward the moment of decision. Far too often I witness salespeople still talking and selling after the prospect has mentally made the purchase. Because they weren't listening with their eyes and ears, these salespeople missed the critical moment to close and so deprived their customers of a comfortable purchase and themselves of a sale. You need to be an effective responsive listener in order to be an effective closer.

The third most important skill is *the ability to sidestep irrelevancies, smoke screens, win/lose games, and manipulative ploys.* Those who have it will always sell more effectively than those who allow themselves to become embroiled in such distractions. People can't help being distracting. Every word I say to you will trigger a unique set of memories in your mind, and unless you really work at preventing it, sooner or later you will be distracted. Even if you are not, you may interpret what I say in a way that is quite different from the meaning I intended.

This is the nature of communication. But the skilled salesperson works to clarify such misunderstandings and digressions, refusing to be tripped up by them. Remember, you are charged with the responsibility to help prospects reach their decisions. It is your task to guide them through the morass of their own thinking, if need be. I have a client who divides the world into "focused thinkers" and "unfocused thinkers." As a professional salesperson you must act as the lens that focuses your customer's thought regardless of whether that customer ends up saying "yes" or "no."

Each of these skills is interrelated with the others. There is a synergy that makes all of them working together much more effective than any one skill would be working alone. Sidestepping is usually best done by asking questions and listening to the answers. It sounds simple and, once you have mastered the skills, it is. It is simply a matter of putting them into practice. However, these skills don't come easily. Each requires extensive daily practice and self-evaluation. This book has provided you with the tools—the rest is up to you.

Throughout this book we have examined many selling techniques and skills. All of them have been presented from the perspective of the customer. The tools of the 1960s and 1970s cannot continue to sell effectively in the 1990s and beyond. What we've learned in the past two decades is that people resist manipulation and demand a sales approach that is more responsive to them personally. I have presented here my concept of buyer-oriented selling because it has been developed and proven to work over the past few years by the thousands of fine salespeople I've trained and worked with. A client of mine once said to his employees: "This company is pulling out of the station. You are either on the train or you will be left standing on the platform." Using the tools I've provided here is hard work. But if you don't want to be left on the platform, put them into practice today, and success will be yours tomorrow. Accept this concept, make these skills your own, practice them, and I can promise you the success you desire in sales in the next two decades.

Appendix

A Selection of Sources of Prospecting Information

Nongovernment Reference Resources

Most of the sources listed here can be found in the reference section of your local public library.

Cole Directory

> Cole Directories
> 529 Fifth Avenue
> New York, N.Y. 10017
> (212) 867-5640

A listing for 1,200 American cities including such information as:

- A street directory
- Buying power section on residential neighborhoods, including wealth ratings, ages, occupancies, and so forth
- Zip Codes
- Office building directory
- Numerical telephone directory (criss-cross)
- Real estate section

- Mailing list information
- Prospecting system for business contacts section

Directories in Print, Fourth Edition

Gale Research Company
Penobscot Building
Detroit, Mich. 48226

A complete listing of all directories of any kind in print. It is divided into categories (such as professional associations, social, business) for easy reference. It can be used to discover further sources of marketing or prospecting information.

Directory of Industrial Data Sources

Harfax Division of Harper & Row
Ballinger Publishing Company
54 Church Street
Cambridge, Mass. 02138
(617) 492-0670

As its name implies, a detailed directory of sources of information on industries.

Dun & Bradstreet State Sales Guide

Dun & Bradstreet
1 Diamond Hill Road
Murray Hill, N.J. 07974

Individual books on each state. Lists companies operating in that state, providing such information as phone numbers, credit rating, years in business, and more.

Dun's Marketing Services

Note: All other Dun & Bradstreet or Dun's publications listed here are available from this address:

Dun's Marketing Services
3 Sylvan Way
Parsippany, N.J. 02054

Dun & Bradstreet Million Dollar and *Billion Dollar Directories*

Detailed information on all companies doing $500,000 or more in business. Includes affiliations, ownership, subsidiaries, and data such as products, officers, address, telephone numbers, and sales volume.

Dun & Bradstreet's Reference Book of Corporate Management

A collection of brief biographical data of top executives.

Dun's Business Ranking

Public and private businesses ranked by industry, category, and state. Includes information such as sales volumes and rank, employee numbers and rank, and SIC Codes.[1]

Dun's Census of American Business

National, state, and county sections. Useful for answering such questions as: How large is the market for my products or services? Where is the greatest concentration of prospects? Who are my competitors in each market?

Dun's Market Identifiers

Similar to the Census of American Business but also includes a three-year business-trend forecast for each company.

The Guide to American Directories

> Klein Publications
> Box 8503
> Coral Springs, Fla. 33005

Alphabetical listing of all directories in print. An excellent resource for additional information sources.

---

[1] An SIC Code (Standard Industrial Classification) is a four-digit number assigned by the U.S. Department of Commerce to identify a specific industry. Every business fits into one or more SIC categories. SIC Codes are useful for finding demographics on companies and for mailing list selection.

Moody's Investors Service

Note: All Moody's products are available from the following address:

Moody's, Inc.
99 Church Street
New York, N.Y. 10007
(212) 553-0300

Moody's Handbook

Quarterly publication that covers over 1,400 publicly held companies. The information includes sales figures, earnings, dividends, and company background.

Moody's Investors Fact Sheets

Business descriptions for over 4,000 publicly held companies, including stock information, financial data, sales by line of business, and a chronological summary of current news items about each company.

Moody's Manuals and News Report

Digests of industrial, municipal, government, bank and finance, public utilities, transportation, and international businesses.

Predicasts F&S Index

Predicasts
11001 Cedar Avenue
Cleveland, Ohio 44106

Index to articles written about specific companies in over 750 periodicals (many of which are available in the library) indexed by industry under SIC Code. The most important stories are indicated by a dot.

PTS Annual Report Abstracts

Predicasts
11001 Cedar Avenue
Cleveland, Ohio 44106

As the name implies, a collection of abstracts of annual reports from publicly owned companies nationwide.

Special Libraries Directory

> Special Libraries Association
> 1700 18th Street, NW
> Washington, D.C. 20009
> (202) 234-4700

A listing of companies and institutions with private libraries. Lists names and phone numbers of librarians, who are usually fine sources of information on their companies and competitors.

Standard and Poor's Registry of Corporations, Directors, and Executives

> Standard and Poor's
> 25 Broadway
> New York, N.Y. 10004

Company name, address, telephone number, products and services, key personnel, number of employees.

Standard Directory of Advertisers

> National Register Publishing Company
> Macmillan, Inc.
> 3004 Glenview Road
> Wilmette, Ill. 60091

A directory of all companies that advertise, with summaries of their current advertising patterns.

Thomas Register of American Manufacturers

> Thomas Publishing Co.
> One Penn Plaza
> New York, N.Y. 10119

> Volumes 1–12: products and services
> Volumes 13–14: company profiles including names, addresses, branch offices, officers, assets, and so forth

Volumes 15–21: catalog file—alphabetically listed companies, cross-referenced, full-page advertisements with detailed company information

Value Line Investment Survey

Arnold Bernhard & Company
711 Third Avenue
New York, N.Y. 10017

Very detailed published summary advice on markets, companies, and industries as well as fact sheets on publicly owned companies.

Wall Street Transcript

Wall Street Journal
99 Wall Street
New York, N.Y. 10005
(212) 747-9500

Features, articles, and studies; also contains broker and information source reports on industries, publicly owned companies, and new securities listings.

Where to Find Business Information

John Wiley & Sons
605 Third Avenue
New York, N.Y. 10158-0012

An excellent reference on how to conduct prospecting/marketing research and where to find information.

Federal Government Sources

Most of these sources publish documents that are available through the U.S. Government Printing Office, Washington, D.C. 20402, (202) 783-3238. In addition, many of them are available in the reference section of your public library.

The Congressional Information Service Index

Superintendent of Documents
U.S. Government Printing Office
Washington, D.C. 20402
(202) 783-3238

Information concerning congressional hearings, investigations, schedules, witnesses, and so forth. An excellent source of detailed information on companies that have been investigated or have appeared before Congress.

Department of Agriculture

> 14th & Independence Avenue, SW
> South Building, Room 5711
> Washington, D.C. 20250
> (202) 447-8999

The National Agriculture Library has an extensive collection of sources on agricultural information. The library also publishes a *Marketing Services Guide* and *Databases Directory*. If you sell to agriculture or the food industry, these should be valuable resources for you.

Department of Commerce, Bureau of Census

> Federal Building #3, Room 2428
> Washington, D.C. 20233
> (202) 763-5662

This is *the* source of market demographics for selling directly to consumers. It segments population regionally by such factors as age, income, family size, religion, property owned.

Internal Revenue Service

> Freedom of Information Reading Room
> 1111 Constitution Avenue, NW
> Washington, D.C. 20224
> (202) 566-3770

Complete financial information on nonprofit organizations.

Securities and Exchange Commission

> Public Reference Section
> Washington, D.C. 20549
> (202) 523-5360

Forms 10K and 10Q providing complete financial information on all publicly held companies.

State and Local Government Sources

All states maintain several different departments that keep records on businesses and individuals under their governance. Among the most helpful are:

Department of Banking
Department of Commerce and Economic Development
Department of Consumer Protection
Department of Environmental Protection
Department of Franchises
Department of Insurance
Department of Labor and Industrial Relations
Department of Motor Vehicles
Food and Drug Administration

Furthermore, most states publish numerous business directories, which are available for the asking.

County Clerk's Office

City governments keep a number of useful records in the county clerk's office. Among the most helpful are:

Construction Permits
Register of Births
Register of Deeds
Register of Marriages
Register of New Businesses
Registry of Leases

Much of this information is published in handy directories available from the local governments.

Information Services

The following is intended only as a representative selection of companies. No endorsement is intended. Entries were selected from various areas around the country.

Capital Systems Group

> 11301 Rockville Pike
> Kensington, Md. 20895
> (301) 881-9400

Infoquest, a commercial and government database, market studies, and so forth.

Dataflow Systems

> 7758 Wisconsin Avenue
> Bethesda, Md. 20014
> (301) 645-9133

Business investigation, market summaries.

Dun & Bradstreet

> 100 Church Street
> New York, N.Y. 10007
> (212) 665-5000 or contact your local office

D&B offers the following services:

- Business Information Reports, which include a rating summary, overview, payments, finance information, history, officers, and operation information
- Analysis Reports
  —Account Analysis (their customers)
  —Market Analysis
  —Market Penetration Reports
  —Market Potential
- Sales Lead Service, a biweekly report of new businesses and ownership changes

Dun's Marketing Services

> Three Century Drive
> Parsippany, N.J. 07054
> 1-800-526-0665

- Dun's Customer Analysis Service, which provides evaluation of your customer base and market potential

- Dun's Market Identifiers, a detailed market data service that helps locate prospects and determine territories
- Dun's Decision Makers List, a detailed list of those identified by job title as key decision makers in companies doing over $500,000 a year in sales
- Dun's Market Research Service, which provides individual research tailored to your market and specifications

Economic Information Systems

310 Madison Avenue
New York, N.Y. 10017
(212) 697-6080

Detailed market surveys, market potential, customer profiles, market penetration analyses, share of market reports, company lines of business reports.

Facts for a Fee

Cleveland Public Library
325 Superior Avenue
Cleveland, Ohio 44114
(216) 623-2999

Competitor profiles, market studies, on-line database searches.

The Information Mart

Box 2400
Santa Barbara, Calif. 93120
(805) 965-5555

Comprehensive computer or manual search on any subject.

Minneapolis Public Library and Information Center

300 Nicollet Mall
Minneapolis, Minn. 55401
(612) 372-6636

Competitor profiles, market studies, industry overviews. Over one hundred databases accessed; corporate and special libraries included.

National Association of Credit Management

811 North Third Street
Phoenix, Ariz. 85004
(602) 252-8866 or contact the local office in your area

Credit ratings and market information.

Schrader Research and Rating Service

South River Road
Cranbury, N.J. 08512
1-800-877-9440

Market research and credit profiles.

TRW Credit Services

Suite 100
505 City Parkway West
Orange, Calif. 92668
(714) 937-2670

Credit ratings and market information.

Washington Researchers

918 16th Avenue
Washington, D.C. 20006
(202) 833-2230

Markets and companies fully researched. Publishers of *How to Find Information About Companies.*

Industrial Research Firms

The Directory of Fee-Based Information Services

Available in most reference libraries or by writing to:

Information Alternative
Box 657
Woodstock, N.Y. 12498

Membership Directory of the Information Industry Association

Information Industry Association
316 Pennsylvania Avenue SE, Suite 400
Washington, D.C. 20003
(202) 544-1969

List Brokers

Local and more regional and national list brokers can be found in the Yellow Pages under the heading "Mailing Lists."

A-Caldwell & Company

2025 Peachtree Street, NE
Atlanta, Ga. 30309
1-800-241-7425

Aetna National List Company

999 East Touhy Avenue
Des Plaines, Ill. 60018
1-800-621-2392

All-Waterbury List

3825 Vinton Avenue
Culver City, Calif. 90232
1-800-331-4710

American Business Lists

5707 South 86th Circle
Omaha, Nebr. 68127
1-800-336-8349

Cole: Target Mailing Lists

> 901 West Bond Street
> Lincoln, Nebr. 68521-9989
> (402) 867-5640

Dun & Bradstreet Credit Services

> 100 Church Street
> New York, N.Y. 10007
> (212) 285-7274

First National List Service

> 2265 West Eastwood Avenue
> Chicago, Ill. 60625
> 1-800-621-5548

Hugo Dunhill Mailing Lists

> 630 Third Avenue
> New York, N.Y. 10017
> 1-800-223-6454

Index

[Italicized page numbers refer to figures.]

ad campaign design, 9–10
affect, 107–108
aggressiveness, 170–174
Agricultural Marketing Service, 34
Agriculture, Department of, 34
anecdote structure to strengthen customer listening, 144
appointment, setting of, 56–57
Aristotle, on persuasion, 140–141
assertive response, 172–173
assertive selling, 170–177
authority, 104–107, 146–147
    justification from, 83–84

behavioral objective, 5–6
body language, 94
businesses, information from, 35–36
buyer's remorse, 99–100
buying life cycles, 18, 161–162

call objectives, 58–70
    alternatives in, 67–68
    clarity of, 168–169, 174–175
canned pitch, 93
cause/effect structure to strengthen customer listening, 143
Census Bureau, 33
change, low tolerance for, 136–137, 153
city government, 32
"closed case" close, 176
closed-ended questions, 116, 118, 119
    disadvantages of, 117–118
closing, 66, 82–84, 168–170
    assertiveness vs. aggressiveness in, 170–174
    from first moment of contact, 167–179
    importance of, 58–59
    with questions, 122–123
    selling skills and, 177–179
    "third party," 144

193

Commerce Department, Bureau
   of Census of, 33
commercial information
   sources, 35–37
commission selling, 41
communication, 93
   language in, 108–110
   nonverbal, 101–108
   in relationships, 108–113
company records, 27–28
competition, activity of, 19
CompuServ, 34
conceptual selling, 12
*Congressional Information
   Service Index,* 33
contrast structure to strengthen
   customer listening, 142
county fairs, 37–38
creative advertising groups, 9–
   10
creative information sources,
   37–38
credibility, 92
cross-reference system, 17–18
customer action, 65–67
customer-centered objectives,
   62–64
customer problems, presenting
   solutions to, 140–152
customers
   abstract view of, 72
   breakdown of list of, 17–20
   causing, to think, 122
   changing attitude of, toward
      product or service, 92–93
   establishing right relation-
      ship with, 85–113
   expression of doubt by, 99–
      100
   finding need of, 74–76
   focus on behavior of, 59

gaining right relationship
   with, 72–74
getting planned response
   from, 62–63
ideal, 9, 13–14
objections of, 78–81
offering, the opportunity to
   buy, 20–21
probing of, 74–75
responsiveness of, 149–152
selection of, 14–16
talking language of, 109–111
timing of selling to, 18–19
view of sellers of, 71–84
see also prospects

danger, defense against, 86
databases, 34–35
decision making, 82–83
   between opposed goals, 125
demographics, 13
desire, recognition of, 82–83
dialogue, rehearsing of, 120
direct mail
   cost of, 40–42
   effectiveness of, 42–44
distractions, ability to sidestep,
   178–179
doubts, overcoming of, 136–137
Dun & Bradstreet, as information source, 34, 36

EASE persuasion, 144–145
ego needs, 129
emotional appeal, 107–108,
   140–141, 145–146
environment, response to, 163
esteem needs, 128–129, 132
ethical appeal, 140–141, 147

failure, reasons for, 4–5
fallback alternatives, 67–68

federal government, information sources of, 33–34
fight or flight reaction, 86
first impressions, 138–139
focus groups, 9–10
force fields, 125–126, 136–137
Freedom of Information Act, 33

gestalt, 142
goals, definition of, 60
Goffman, Erving, on role playing, 95
government information sources, 31–32
Government Printing Office, U.S., 33

Hertzberg, Frederick, on worker motivation, 130–131, 133

industrial research firms, 35, 36–37, 190–191
information
from questions, 121–122
as source of power, 160–162
information services, 187–190
information sources, 23–38
government, 185–187
industrial research firm, 190–191
from information services, 187–190
list broker, 191–192
nongovernment, 180–185
Internal Revenue Service, 34

justification, 141, 146–147
from authorities, 83–84

language, and relationships, 108–113

lead-swapping network, 25–27
letters, effective, 43, *44,* 45–46
Lewin, Kurt, on motivation, 124–126
Lexis, 34–35
library, prospecting from, 31
list brokers, 35–36, 191–192
listening ability, 76, 178
logical appeal, 83, 140–145
lose/lose game, 89
losing face, fear of, 137

magazines, 32–33
mailing lists, 10
mailings, 40–46
cost of, 40
effectiveness of, 42–46
management/labor disputes, 90
manipulation, mistrust of, 93
market, size and scope of, 10
market information, for effective prospecting, 39–57
marketing, 9
approach to, 22–38
creative groups in, 9–10
five steps to, 11–21
market segment, 10
Maslow, Abraham, needs hierarchy of, 126, *127,* 128–130
mass marketing, *see* direct mail
math teacher syndrome, 77
Mead Data Central, database of, 34–35
metaphors, spotting of, 109–110
misunderstandings, ability to clarify, 178–179
Moody's, database of, 34
motivating factors, 133–134
motivation, 124–125
factors in, 130–131
and needs hierarchy, 126–130

needs, general and customer,
    79, 140
  questions to explore, 124–133
  unawareness of, 123–124
needs hierarchy, 126, *127,* 128–
    130
needs satisfaction selling, 74–76
negotiating solutions to custom-
    ers' problems, 153–166
negotiation stage, 159–163
newspapers, 32–33
Nierenberg, Gerard, and his five
    uses for questions, 121
nonverbal behavior, 101–108
nonzero/sum game, 89
"not interested" objection, 164
"not now" objection, 164
"not right" objection, 164–165

objections
  from fear or uncertainty, 81
  motivations for, 78
  need to confront, frankly, 106
  need to question, 175
  negotiation of, 78–81, 163–
    166
  reasons for, 153
  response to, 156–159
  smoke screen vs. real, 154–
    156
  sources of, 79–80
objectives, 60–64, 68
  clarity of, 69–70
  customer-centered, 62–64
  fallback alternatives, 67–68
  writing down of, 61–62
on-line databases, 34–35
open-ended questions, 114, 118–
    119
  advantages of, 117–118
options, negotiation of, 80

passive-aggressive response, 172
passive response, 171–172
peer pressure, 137–138
persistence, 161
personal information sources,
    24–30
persuasion, 140–141
  through authority, 146–147
  emotion in, 107–108, 145–146
  logical, 141–145
  rationale for, 66–67
phone calls, *see* telephone calls
physiological needs, 127–128
Poor Richard's Almanac, sales
    technique in, 80
precedent, authority of, 105
predictability need, 86–88
predictability principle, 86–89
  and win/win attitude, 91–92
presentation matrix, 149, *150,*
    151–152
press, information from, 32–33
price objection, 165–166
probability game, 89
probing, reaction to, 75
problem/solution structure to
    strengthen customer listen-
    ing, 142–143
Prodigy, 34
product
  customers' attitude toward,
    92–93, 136
  specification of, 11–14
product knowledge, 12, 162
  and technical language, 147–
    148
progressive order structure to
    strengthen customer listen-
    ing, 143–144
prospecting, 8–9
  effective use of market infor-
    mation for, 39–57

information sources for, 23–38, 180–192

versus marketing, 8–21

prospects

breakdown of lists of, 17–18

defensiveness of, 88–89

"good potential" or "interested," 27

nonbuying contacts of, 29–30

objectives of, 93–94

profile of, 9

putting list of, to work, 39–40

qualifying of, from source material, 17–20

readiness to buy, 4–5

research sources for, 16–17

steps to contacting of, 40

uninterested, 27–28

see also customers

public information sources, 30–35

Question Game, 120–121

question reflex, 120–121

questions, 114–119

ability to ask, 177–178

attentiveness to answers to, 75–76

closed-ended, 116–117

in closing, 122–123

and control, 114

customer attitude toward, 75

to explore needs, 124–133

formats for, 116–119

hostility and resistance to, 115–116

how to use, 121–123

irrelevant, 115

open-ended, 106, 116–119

reasons for, 121–133

steps to improvement of, 119–121

to uncover objections, 133–139, 157

writing down, 119

rapport, establishment of, 72–74, 85–113

rational appeal, 140–145

rationalizations, 83

referrals, prospecting from, 28–29

relationships, 5

vs. content, in selling, 94–100

establishment of, 85–113

language and, 108–113

research sources, 16–20

resistance

questions to uncover, 133–139

reasons for, 134–139

responsiveness, 102–104

lack of, 102–103

R. L. Polk & Company, 36

role playing, 95–99

safety needs, 128

sale, closing of, 82–84

sales call, steps in, 71–84

sales goals, 15–16

sales managers, complaints of, 58–59

salespeople

how buyers see, 71–84

negative stereotype of, 73, 88–89

sales presentation, 147–149

as dialogue vs. monologue, 76

features, advantages, benefits model of, 77–78

matrix of, 149, *150*, 151–152

from seller's vs. customer's knowledge base, 76–77

satisfiers, 133, 134

screening person, dealing with
  in telephone calls, 51–52
Securities and Exchange Commission, 34
self-actualization needs, 129–
  130
self-disclosure, 135, 158–159
self-interest, parochial, 134–135
self-testing, 177
selling
  and behavioral objective of
    sales call, 5–6
  content vs. relationship in,
    94–100
  and needs, 129–130, 132–133
  negotiation stage of, 159–163
  plays going on in, 96–99
  sources of power or leverage
    in, 160–161
  timing of, 18–19
  with win/lose attitude, 90–91
selling cycle, 71–84
selling skills, 177–179
sensory biases, 110–112
service, *see* product
social needs, 128–129, 132
solutions
  negotiation of, 153–166
  presentation of, 76–78
Standard & Poor's, database of,
  34
star performers, mind-set of,
  59–60
state government, information
  sources of, 32
status messages, 105

stereotyping, 87–88
  breaking of, 91–94
stock prices, 38
structural patterns, 142–144

technical language, 147–148
technique, 163
telephone calls, 46, 107
  action step in, 56–57
  answers to objections during,
    48–49
  clarity of, 47–48
  flow of, *50*
  how to conduct, 49–57
  objective of, 47
  preparation for, 46–49
  reading scripts for, 47
  reason statement for, 47–48
  secretaries and, 51–52
test market area, 10–11
"third party close," 144
time, as power source, 160–161
trust, 93–94, 158–159
  lack of, on the part of the
    prospect, 135–136

uncertainty, 81

Value Line, 34
von Neuman, John, probability
  game of, 89

win/win attitude, 89–94

Yellow Pages, 30–31

zero/sum playing, 89–94